BRIGHT NOTES

THE MAN WITHOUT A COUNTRY BY EDWARD EVERETT HALE

Intelligent Education

Nashville, Tennessee

BRIGHT NOTES: The Man Without a Country
www.BrightNotes.com

No part of this publication may be used or reproduced in any manner whatsoever without written permission, except in the case of brief quotations in critical articles and reviews. For permissions, contact Influence Publishers http://www.influencepublishers.com.

ISBN: 978-1-645420-96-5 (Paperback)
ISBN: 978-1-645420-97-2 (eBook)

Published in accordance with the U.S. Copyright Office Orphan Works and Mass Digitization report of the register of copyrights, June 2015.

Originally published by Monarch Press.
Eric J Solibakke, 1966
2019 Edition published by Influence Publishers.

Interior design by Lapiz Digital Services. Cover Design by Thinkpen Designs.

Printed in the United States of America.

Library of Congress Cataloging-in-Publication Data forthcoming.
Names: Intelligent Education
Title: BRIGHT NOTES: The Man Without a Country
Subject: STU004000 STUDY AIDS / Book Notes

CONTENTS

1)	Introduction to Edward Everett Hale	1
2)	Textual Analysis	
	Part 1	15
	Part 2	34
	Part 3	53
	Part 4	71
	Part 5	76
3)	Analyses of Characters	95
4)	Critical Review	102
5)	Essay Questions and Answers	111
6)	Bibliography	117

INTRODUCTION TO EDWARD EVERETT HALE

Edward Everett Hale (1822-1909) was a famous Unitarian minister, a popular writer, and a man very much interested in the welfare of his country and the American people. He was a member of an old New England family, but did not feel that the old families should rule the United States. He was interested in the section of the country in which he was born and lived, but he visited and wrote about other sections of the country also. His many articles and books covered a wide range of subjects. He wrote novels, short stories, biographies, autobiographical works, works on theology, travel books, and works on the settlement of the West. He was, in addition, a famous preacher. His most famous work, however, is *The Man Without a Country*, an historical short story which praises patriotism and condemns those who put local or selfish interest ahead of the welfare of America.

EARLY LIFE

Hale was born April 3, 1822, in Boston, Massachusetts. His father, Nathan Hale, was the editor of the *Boston Daily Advertiser*. The father was named after his own uncle, Captain Nathan Hale (1755-1776), the American patriot who was hanged by the British as a spy during the Revolutionary War. Captain Hale is remembered as the man who said, just before he was hanged, "I only regret than I have but one life to lose for my country." His mother, Sarah Everett, was an educated woman and translated books and magazine articles from foreign languages into English. Edward Everett Hale was named after his mother's older brother, Edward Everett, minister of a Unitarian church in Boston. Hale inherited from his parents his love of learning, his religious devotion, and his patriotism.

He was only two years old when he started to school. He attended two small grammar schools until he was nine. At that time he transferred to the Latin School, a high school which stressed Greek and Roman culture. In 1835, at the age of 13, he entered Harvard College he graduated four years later. One of his teachers at Harvard was Henry Wadsworth Longfellow, the famous American poet. One of his classmates at Harvard was James Russell Lowell, the famous American poet, critic, and author. After his graduation in 1839, he studied for the ministry and was licensed as a Unitarian minister in 1842, at the age of 21. He preached in various places, but in 1856 he was appointed minister of the South Congregational Church in Boston. He remained there until 1899. He was named as chaplain of the United States Senate in 1903 and kept this post until his death in 1909.

HIS INTEREST IN WRITING

Since childhood Hale had been interested in literature and writing. While at college he wrote for a college quarterly and he had contributed articles to his father's newspaper. After graduation from college, he began to write reviews and articles for various magazines, such as the *Atlantic Monthly*. His first successful story, "My Double and How He Undid Me," was published in the Atlantic in 1859. As the teller of this story, Hale pretends that he is a minister by the name of Frederic Ingham. He used this nom de plume or pen name to disguise his identity in writing a number of stories. Frederic Ingham, in these stories, is not very much like the real Edward Everett Hale and he is not always described the same way. In *The Man Without a Country*, for example, Frederic Ingham is not a minister, but a retired Navy captain. Hale thought that *In His name* (1874), an historical novel about Italian Protestants of the 12th century, was his best work. Other works are *If, Yes, and Perhaps* (1868), a collection of tales; *Ten Times One Is Ten* (1871), a short novel; and *Franklin in France* (1887–1888), an account of Benjamin Franklin's diplomatic mission to France. *Readers of The Man Without a Country* (1863) would also be interested in *Philip Nolan's Friends* (1876), a novel based on the life of an adventurer who was killed in Texas in 1801.

OPPOSITION TO SLAVERY

The Man Without a Country reflects to a limited extent the wide range of Hale's interests and also many of his ideals. Hale was opposed to slavery. This short story describes some of the evils of slavery. Vaughan, a United States Navy officer is made angry by the discovery of Africans in chains aboard a slave ship. He promises to hang the men who enslaved them. Hale always believed that Negroes are as intelligent as whites and he took an active interest in the education of freed slaves after the Civil War. Hale also supported the Massachusetts Emigrant Aid Company, an organization which recruited settlers for the new territories in the West. He was anxious that these settlers be opposed to slavery. Philip Nolan hears with delight Ingham's account of the movement of American pioneers into Texas and California.

Later in life Hale visited both Texas and California and wrote about his travels there.

OPPOSITION TO BIGOTRY

Hale was opposed to religious and racial bigotry also. He preached against those who had prejudices against Irish, Polish, and other immigrants. He felt that these Europeans, no matter what their language or religion was, should become part of the United States and he was anxious to see them settle in the West. Although Hale was a Unitarian minister, Philip Nolan appears to be a Presbyterian and Danforth an Episcopalian. Like Hale, his fictional Philip Nolan is a religious man. Hale worked for the relief of Irish Catholics during the great Potato Famine of 1846–1848. The Negroes in *The Man Without a Country* are described in sympathetic and human terms. The African slaves are described as men with the same longings for home and family that all men have.

HALE'S INTEREST IN HISTORY

Hale did not serve in either the Army or Navy, but he was interested in both services. He wrote "The Naval History of the American Revolution" and an article on "Paul Jones and Denis Duval." Paul Jones is often called the Father of the American Navy. He spent several weeks, in a civilian capacity, during the Civil War, in an army camp. This was, however, a year after he wrote his account of Philip Nolan, a former lieutenant of the United States Army. Hale was always interested in the history of the United States and he wrote, with the help of Sydney Gay, a *Popular History of the United States* (1877). *His Memories of a Hundred Years* is both a collection of family and personal memories and a history of the United States from 1800 to 1900. *The Man Without a Country* is, in very abbreviated form, a history of the United States from 1801 to 1863.

VIEWS ON JEFFERSON

The Memories of Hale and his *The Man Without a Country* show his strong bias against Jefferson. Hale believed in a strong Navy and Jefferson did not. Hale thought that Jefferson and other presidents who came from Virginia did not do enough to put an end to the slave trade. In 1803, during Jefferson's presidency, the United States bought the territory called the Louisiana Purchase and in doing so almost doubled the size of the United States. Hale believed very much in the expansion of the United States, but he says nothing about Jefferson's part in this purchase. Madison is also attacked for his failure to hold Nuku-Hiva Island in the Pacific. Captain Porter held it briefly during the War of 1812. Four of the first five presidents of the United States were from wealthy Virginian families. Hale felt that it was not good for democracy for so many presidents to come from the same area and the same class. Both Ingham and Nolan attack these presidents in *The Man Without a Country*. Washington, our first president, was from Virginia, but Hale never attacks him. Hale does not mention the fact that John Adams, the 2nd President of the United States, was the father of John Quincy Adams, the 6th President. The Adams were from New England.

HALE'S PATRIOTISM

Hale's devotion to America, his patriotism, was really a devotion to an ideal. He believed that Americans should know their history, that all men should be free and equal, and that

Americans should love and serve their country. Patriotism to Hale was both a religious and a romantic ideal. The country deserves love even when the patriot is not rewarded and a man should love America the way he loves his wife.

LATER LIFE

His own life was peaceful and happy. Hale's parents were kind and understanding and his brothers and sisters and he were close to one another. He married Emily Perkins in 1845. Their family life was very happy and both lived to see their one daughter and four sons lead successful lives. Hale's books, especially *The Man Without a Country*, were very popular and he was widely recognized throughout the country as a literary man and as a preacher. When he died on June 10, 1909, he was praised everywhere as a preacher, a writer, and a patriot.

HISTORICAL BACKGROUND

Events in *The Man Without a Country* take place between 1805 and 1863. There are also a number of references to events that took place before that time. In order to fully understand Hale's story a review of the historical events of the period is necessary.

In the Declaration of Independence of 1776, the people of the thirteen colonies in America explained why they should be free from England. These colonies, with the help of France, won their independence when Cornwallis surrendered at Yorktown in 1781. The Constitution of the United States was finally ratified by the thirteen states in 1788 and the next year George Washington was inaugurated as the first President (1789–1797). John Adams, the second President (1797–1801) resisted French efforts to control American trade and as a result there were many battles between French and American ships from 1798 to 1800. War was never declared, however.

During the administration of Jefferson, the third President (1801–1809), the American Navy defeated the pirates of North Africa in the Barbary Wars (1801–1805). Jefferson doubled the size of the United States when he made the Louisiana Purchase from Napoleon in 1803. Jefferson authorized the Lewis and Clark Expedition (1804–1806) to explore the American West and in 1808 Congress forbade the further importation of slaves. Aaron Burr attempted to seize control of some territories in the West in order to establish a personal empire. He was stopped by President Jefferson and tried for treason in Richmond, Virginia in 1807. he was acquitted.

When James Madison was President (1809–1817), America fought the War of 1812 (1812–1814) against England in order to protect American ships from seizure and search by the English Navy. During this war, the United States ship Constitution, under the command of Captain Isaac Hull, defeated the English ship Guerriere. Later, under the command of Captain William Bainbridge, the Constitution seized the English ship Java. Captain David Porter of the Essex captured the Alert and nine other vessels. He sailed into the Pacific Ocean and took possession of Nuku-Hiva Island for the United States. In 1814 General Ross of the English Army captured the capital city of Washington and set fire to all public buildings. America and England signed the Treaty of Ghent in 1814. They agreed to stop fighting and promised to hunt out and punish anyone engaged in the slave trade. Unaware of this treaty, General Andrew Jackson defeated an English military force in the Battle of New Orleans in 1815, 15 days after the treaty was signed.

Mexico won her independence from Spain in 1821. James Monroe was President (1817-1825) at that time. The next year Stephen Fuller Austin began to settle Americans in Texas, which was then a part of Mexico. In 1836, when Andrew Jackson was President (1829-1837), the Americans in Texas freed themselves from the rule of Mexico and established an independent republic. James K. Polk was President (1845-1849) when Texas was admitted to the Union as a state in 1845. The Mexican War (1846-1848) ended in American victory. General Zachary Taylor led an American army into Mexico. By the Treaty of Guadalupe Hidalgo, America got possession of California, Nevada, Utah, and parts of Texas and New Mexico. America acquired, by peaceful settlement with England, sole possession of the Oregon Territory in 1846. In 1860 Abraham Lincoln was elected President (1861-1865). When he took office, 11 southern states declared themselves separated from the United States. They established for themselves a new government called the Confederate States of America. The Civil War or the War Between the States then followed. General Ulysses S. Grant, who was commander of Union forces in the West, cut the Confederate States in two when he seized Vicksburg, Mississippi on July 4, 1863. He later became commander-in-chief of all Union forces. The western counties of Virginia which refused to leave the Union were separated from Virginia and admitted as the 35th state in 1863.

BRIEF PLOT SUMMARY

Frederic Ingham does not tell the story of Philip Nolan in proper order. He skips back and forth in time and once in a while he contradicts himself. The following brief summary gives the outline of the plot in proper order.

THE MAN WITHOUT A COUNTRY

Philip Nolan was born about 1783 in Kentucky and he was brought up on a plantation. He received little formal education and frequently went with his older brother Stephen to Texas to hunt wild horses. He enlisted in the Army around 1800, and he met Aaron Burr for the first time in 1805, probably at Fort Massac, in what is today southern Illinois. He agreed to help Aaron Burr seize some of the western territories of the United States in order to set up a separate empire. He met Burr around August of 1806, when Burr came west to begin his rebellion. In 1807, both Burr and Nolan were tried for treason. Burr was tried in Richmond, Virginia, but he was found innocent. Nolan was tried by the Army at Fort Adams, Mississippi. He was found guilty. The sentence was given by Colonel Morgan on September 23, 1807. Nolan was told that he was never again to hear of the United States. He was taken by military escort down the Mississippi River to New Orleans and put aboard the Navy ship Nautilus. President Jefferson in Washington approved of this sentence. Between 1807 and 1810, the Nautilus stopped at the Cape of Good Hope in South Africa. Nolan became embarrassed and angry while reading *The Lay of the Last Minstrel* aloud. He threw the book into the ocean. About 1810, he was transferred from the Nautilus to the Warren somewhere near the Windward Islands. Between 1810 and 1812, he met Mrs. Graff, and old friend, at a dance while the Warren was anchored in the Bay of Naples. She refused to talk about the United States with him. It is said that Burr and Nolan once met in the Mediterranean at this time, but Ingham does not believe this story. Nolan next appeared aboard the Constitution, which was under the command of Captain Bainbridge. On December 29, 1812, Nolan took command of a gun in a sea battle with the English ship Java. Bainbridge gave Nolan his sword. Before the Constitution sailed north, Nolan was transferred to the Essex under the command of Captain David Porter. Porter then sailed around Cape Horn into the Pacific and occupied Nuku-Hiva Island from October to December of 1813. Captain Bainbridge mentioned Nolan in his report when he returned to Washington. The Navy Department at this time began to claim that Nolan did not exist. Nolan's records were lost in 1814 when General Ross set fire to Washington's public buildings. After 1817, when Monroe was President, Nolan is never again mentioned in an official report.

Between 1820 and 1822, Nolan was aboard a ship which was patrolling the western coast of Africa. He was asked to translate for an officer who had taken charge of a captured slave ship. At the same time, Nolan became the close friend of a young midshipman by the name of Frederic Ingham. Shortly after that, Ingham heard the account of Nolan throwing *The Lay of the Last Minstrel* into the sea. Ingham was visiting Cairo and the Pyramids at the time. About 1823 or 1825, Ingham left Nolan while their ship was anchored off St. Thomas in the West Indies. They met again in 1830, but we are not told on what ship. When they met aboard the Intrepid around 1837, Ingham was the 2nd officer. It is then that Ingham read for the first time the original instructions governing Nolan's imprisonment. Sometime later, probably after 1841, Ingham and Nolan met aboard the George Washington. Ingham was the captain of that ship. In 1945, when Texas had just been admitted to the Union, some officers discussed whether or not to cut Texas out of Nolan's maps. Lt. Truxton, who was present during the discussion, later told Ingham about it. Nolan and Ingham did not see one another after that, but Ingham wrote Nolan twice a year. We do not know how much longer he did so. Other officers observed at this time that Nolan aged very fast during these years.

Nolan died on May 11, 1863, aboard the Levant. News of his death was printed in the New York Herald on August 13, 1863.

A week or so later, Frederic Ingham, who was waiting for a steamer in Mackinaw City, Michigan, read this new item. He then wrote the story of Philip Nolan. Soon after he received a letter from Danforth, written the day after Nolan's death.

HISTORICAL FICTION

Fiction is any story (novel, short story, etc.) in which the events and characters are imaginary rather than true. Historical fiction mixes both the imaginary and the historical. Many of the characters and events in this story are true, but others are imaginary. *The Man Without a Country* is historical fiction. It is a short story in which the "hero" and two other main characters are imaginary. And, of course, the plot is also imaginary. One of the important characters, however, is a real historical person. So are a number of other minor characters. Aaron Burr's story as related in *The Man Without a Country* is essentially true. Since Philip Nolan is an imaginary character, the account of Aaron Burr's relationship with him is also imaginary, not historical. All the background is essentially true. For example, the frigate-duel between the Constitution and the Java and Porter's seizure of Nuku-Hiva are historical events. Nolan's part in these events, however, is fictional.

It is the purpose of any writer of fiction to make his reader believe that his story is true. Hale does this in several ways. First of all, he is careful to relate Nolan's story to historical events and real persons. Almost all the minor characters are given names which sound familiar to anyone who knows American history. These minor characters are usually fictional, however. For example, the Mrs. Graff that Nolan dances with aboard the Warren was a Miss Rutledge before she married. She is a fictional character, but both Graff and Rutledge are family names that have been important since the American Revolution. In the same way, ships are given names that sound familiar. Some ships, like the Constitution and the Java, are real ships. Most of the others, however, are fictional. The Levant, for example, was once a Navy ship, but when this story was written it had already been lost at sea for two years. It must, therefore, be considered a fictional ship. The most important way to make fiction seem true is by creating people that act the way ordinary people do. Frederic Ingham, for example, tries to tell the story of Philip Nolan. Ingham is an old retired naval officer and some of the events he talks about happened over 50 years before. Moreover, he was not present when most of the things he talks about took place. It is not surprising, therefore, that Ingham makes mistakes, contradicts himself, or is unsure of his facts. Ingham does not sound like a professional writer who can organize a story properly. For example, he is not sure who the commander of the Nautilus was or who was Secretary of the Navy when Nolan was sentenced. Later on he decides that Shaw was the commander.

MYSTERY AND TRAGEDY

There are frequent changes and confusions in time in this story. The plot, therefore, appears to be very complicated. That which unifies the story is the character of Philip Nolan and the mystery surrounding him. *The Man Without a Country* is the story of a man who has betrayed his country and is given a sentence of lifelong exile aboard ships of the United States Navy. No one is permitted to speak to him about the United States. He is defiant at first, but later he becomes shy and seems to be a broken man. He proves his devotion to his country in war, but all efforts to free him seem hopeless. The story as told by Ingham is a tragic one. That is, Nolan is the victim of forces that are too strong for him and he is crushed by these forces. As Ingham sees it, Nolan had paid for his crime of treason and he deserved to be set free. However, the red tape of government bureaucracy in the Navy Department allowed Nolan to spend the rest of his life imprisoned aboard ship.

Danforth's letter changes Nolan's story from tragedy to a story with a happy ending and solves a mystery connected with Nolan. For the most of his life, Nolan spent a good part of his time in his stateroom and no one was permitted to enter it. This is one of the mysteries surrounding him. He is also made mysterious simply because he is an unusual person. The stateroom, Danforth writes, is actually filled with symbols of the United States. The mystery of his stateroom is solved. Nolan spent most of his life praying for his country and helping young seamen. He declared on his death bed that he died a happy man and is made further happy by news of the growth of the United States.

STYLE

The style of that part of the short story written by Ingham is colloquial. He uses exaggeration sometimes, foreign words on occasion, and **irony**. Colloquial means the language used in conversation. It is, of course, very good English. Expressions like "By Jove" and "Well" are used in good conversation, but they are not ordinarily written down in formal compositions. When Ingham says that the Negroes aboard the slave ship were speaking in "every dialect and patois of a dialect," he is using exaggeration. He only means that they were speaking more than one language. When Ingham says that it is perhaps right that Burr and other important leaders of the plot against the United States were let go, he is using **irony**. We know this is so because he frequently condemns Burr and describes him as the "gay deceiver" and says that he corrupted Philip Nolan.

TONE

The tone is for the most part sad, but there are moments of hope, mystery, and excitement to relieve this mood. It is sad because of Nolan. The reader feels sorry for Nolan because he is lonely and forgotten. Some hope is raised when he proves his bravery and devotion in the frigate-duel and Bain-bridge tries to get him released. There was excitement when Nolan attended the dance on the Warren. Both the excitement and hope give way to sadness, however. Nolan's kindness to Ingham, Danforth, and others draws the reader's sympathy for Nolan and increases the mood of sadness.

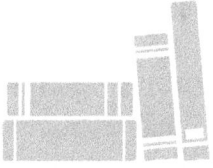

THE MAN WITHOUT A COUNTRY

TEXTUAL ANALYSIS

PART 1

ANNOUNCEMENT OF NOLAN'S DEATH

Frederic Ingham, the man who tells this story, says he read a notice of the death of Philip Nolan in the August 13, 1863, issue of the New York Herald. According to this announcement, Philip Nolan died on May 11, 1863, aboard the corvette Levant, a United States Navy vessel. The ship at the time of Nolan's death was in the middle of the Pacific Ocean. Ingham believes that few people would have read this notice as it was in the back of the newspaper.

Comment

In this paragraph, Edward Everett Hale introduces both the narrator (the man who tells the story) and the subject of his story. He gives many details which make this story seem true. He also gives a hint, to those who know their naval history, that it is not a true story.

Here and throughout the story, Hale gives very particular information and uses real names to make his story seem true. For example, the *New York Herald* was a real newspaper. It is now known as the *New York Herald-Tribune*. There was a famous corvette by the name of Levant. The exact location of the ship is given. Ships give their positions by latitude and longitude and the position of the Levant can easily be traced on a map. The latitude is two degrees, 11 minutes South and the longitude is 131 degrees West. That would locate the ship just below the Equator and midway between the Hawaiian Islands and Mexico.

Hale used the name Levant to indicate that his story is not true. The United States Navy corvette Levant was lost at sea two years before Nolan's death. Hale thought that some readers in 1863 would remember this. He says that in his first version of the story, he gave lines of longitude and latitude which would put the ship on the top of the Andes Mountains in South America. This would have been a second hint that the story is not true. Hale also thought it would be amusing to put a ship on a mountain top. However, due to the care of a proofreader or an editor or due to his own carelessness, the position of the Levant was changed to put it in the middle of the ocean rather than on a mountain.

CHARACTER ANALYSIS

Frederic Ingham is called either "Fred" or "Ingham." He was only a young midshipman when he first met Nolan after the War of 1812. He claims that he was one of the Nolan's favorite friends. He served aboard ships where Nolan was imprisoned three or more times. He used to write him twice a year even though Nolan never replied. He tried without success to get the Navy to free Nolan. He was 2nd officer aboard the Intrepid about 1837, and

Nolan was then attached to his ship. He was later captain of the George Washington about 1841, and Nolan was also confined to that ship. At the time he writes this story, Ingham is a retired Navy captain and he is about 60 years old.

NOTES

A Corvette in Hale's time was a sailing vessel. It was smaller than a frigate and it had only one row of guns, usually 20 or less.

Latitude: On flat maps, these are the lines running from East to West.

Longitude: On flat maps, these are the lines running from North to South.

INGHAM REMEMBERS NOLAN

Frederic Ingham was stranded at the Old Mission-House in Mackinaw City, Michigan, when he read the announcement of Nolan's death in the newspaper. He could not leave until the arrival of the next Lake Superior steamer. In order to kill time, he read all the magazines and newspapers he could find. That is why he even read the announcements of deaths and marriages in the *New York Herald*. Ingham claims that he has a good memory for people and names. He has a special reason to remember Philip Nolan. Hundreds of others would have noticed the announcement of Philip Nolan's death if he had been identified as "the man without a country." During the 50 years of Nolan's exile, many officers who served aboard the ship where he was confined did not even know his name. He was generally known only as "the man without a country."

Comment

Hale now introduces the **theme** or subject of his story and Ingham says that he is especially qualified to tell the story. The **theme** or subject of the story is the very unusual one of a man who does not have a country. The rest of the story explains this mysterious title. Ingham prides himself on his ability to remember people and names. The reader who pays attention will be amused to notice that later on Ingham's memory is not as good as he thinks it is. For example, he cannot remember whether it was Tingey or Shaw who was in command of the ship to which Nolan was first assigned. He is not sure which of the Crowninshields was Secretary of the Navy after the War of 1812. He is not sure whether it was Tucker or Watson who had command of Nolan at the end of the War of 1812.

When Ingham reads the announcement of Nolan's death, the American Civil War was already two years in progress. The fact that Ingham is in remote Mackinaw City indicates that he is no longer in the Navy.

NOTES

Civil War or the War Between The States lasted from 1861 to 1865. Later on Nolan's friend Danforth will speak of this war as the "infernal Rebellion."

Mackinaw is present day Mackinaw City, as village on the southern shore of the Strait of Mackinac in northern Michigan. The Jesuits in the 17th and 18th centuries had an Indian mission in this area. That is why the hotel or lodgings where Ingham is staying is called Mission-House.

Three-Years Cruise. In Ingham's time, a Navy officer would ordinarily serve aboard a ship for a period of three years.

NAVY DEPARTMENT DOES NOT KNOW NOLAN

Ingham says that there can be no harm in telling the full story of poor Nolan. There had been reason before this. Ever since the administration of President Madison, Nolan's story had been kept secret. He congratulates the officers of the Navy for keeping this secret. It proves that they have been both honorable as individuals and as Navy officers. When Ingham was attached to the Bureau of Construction in Washington, he looked through the records in the Naval Archives. As a result he came to the conclusion that every official report relating to Nolan had been burned when General Ross set fire to the public buildings in Washington. At the end of the War of 1812, one of the Tuckers, or perhaps one of the Watsons, was commander of the ship on which Nolan was imprisoned. When this commander reported to the Secretary of the Navy, he found that the Navy Department did not know anything about Nolan. Ingham is not sure which of the Crowninshields was Secretary of the Navy at the time. He is not sure that the Navy knew anything about Nolan. Perhaps they only pretended not to know about him as a matter of policy. In any case, ever since 1817, no naval officer ever mentioned Nolan when filing a report to the Navy Department at the end of a three-year cruise.

Comment

Ingham here explains why no one knows Nolan by name. Ingham's memory fails him when he tries to recall some important names. Hale has included a deliberate piece of misinformation as another hint to his readers that this is not a true story. His congratulations to the officers of the Navy is ironic. Hale gives the story an historical basis by his reference to real people and to an **episode** in the War of 1812.

The full **irony** of Ingham's congratulations will not be seen clearly until later on in the story. **Irony** in the simplest form means that the author wants the reader to understand that he means the exact opposite of what he says. When Hale, in this patriotic story, praises Navy officers for their enthusiastic devotion to their duty, he means exactly what he says. However, he is ironic when he has Ingham praise them for pretending to know nothing about Nolan. Later on in the story, Ingham will make it clear that he himself worked hard to free Nolan from lifelong imprisonment. It is this very secrecy that he praises which keeps him from succeeding. Both Ingham and Hale agree that Nolan's treason deserves punishment. Later on, however, when Nolan has been punished and definitely proved himself to be a loyal and patriotic American, there is no longer any reason for his harsh imprisonment. This praising of Navy secrecy in the case of Nolan is also an ironic attack on bureaucracy. If Nolan's records were lost, then Nolan was a victim of government workers who were too lazy or too inhuman to care what happened to him. If they are not lost, he was the victim of government workers who do not know how to handle a case not covered by regulations.

As already pointed out, Ingham's memory for names and people is not as good as he claims it is. He has confused in his mind the Tuckers and the Watsons and he is not sure which of the Crowninshields was Secretary of the Navy. All these are names of real people attached to the Navy during this period. There were two Crowninshields who were Secretary of the Navy. These names, the name of President Madison, and the reference to the burning of Washington by General Ross give the story authenticity (**realism**), because all are historical.

As Hale well knew, however, it is unlikely that Nolan's records were destroyed by General Ross. Just before General Ross's attack on Washington, all public documents and the Naval Archives were removed from Washington by boat up the Potomac River for safety. Ross took Washington on August 24, 1814, and that same night and the following day his men set fire to all the public buildings, including the halls of Congress, the Supreme Court Building, public offices, and the Naval Archives. However, the documents and records in the Naval Archives had already been removed to safety between August 21st to 23rd. This is another of Hale's indications that his story is fictional.

NOTES

Madison's Administration refers to James Madison (1751–1836) who was President from March 4, 1809, to March 3, 1817.

War Of 1812: The United States declared war on Great Britain in June, 1812, and the war ended in December, 1814, with the Treaty of Ghent. America declared war because (1) English ships were illegally searching American vessels and seizing sailors, (2) Americans thought that the English were encouraging Indians to attack American settlers in the West, (3) many Americans wanted to seize western territories held by England. Danforth later on refers to this war as "the English war."

General Robert Ross (1766–1814): His troops occupied the capital of the United States for two days and set fire to all public buildings. He instructed his troops not to harm civilians or damage private property. He was killed on September 12, 1814, in an unsuccessful attempt to seize Baltimore, Maryland.

Crowninshields: There were two men by this name who were Secretary of the Navy. Jacob Crowninshield (1770-1808) was appointed Secretary of the Navy by President Jefferson (1801-1808), but he never wanted this position and never assumed office. He died before the War of 1812 and could not be the Secretary of the Navy that Ingham has in mind. His brother, Benjamin W. Crowninshield (1772-1851) was Secretary of the Navy from 1814 to 1818. He would have been the Secretary to whom Nolan's commanding officer would have reported. Although Ingham cannot remember clearly which of the brothers was Secretary of the Navy some 49 years earlier, Edward Everett Hale, who wrote "The Naval History of the American Revolution," would have known which Crowninshield held office at that time.

Esprit De Corps is a French expression which means enthusiastic devotion to duty. Here it specifically refers to devotion to the Navy and the feeling of loyalty which all the Navy officers had towards the Navy and one another.

Non Mi Ricordo is an Italian expression which means "I do not remember." Ingham suspects, but is not certain, that it was official naval policy to claim that no one remembered anything about Philip Nolan.

MORAL OF NOLAN'S STORY

Because Nolan is now dead, there is no longer reason to be secret about his story. Ingham intends to tell the story of Philip Nolan so that young Americans will know what it is to be "a man without a country."

Comment

Notice that so far Hale has not explained why Nolan was "a man without a country." He has withheld this information, because he wants the reader to first feel sorry for Nolan. Notice that he refers to him as a "poor wretch" and a "poor creature."

NOLAN MEETS AARON BURR

Philip Nolan was a fine young officer in the western division of the United States Army. That division was called the "Legion of the West." When Aaron Burr made his spectacular trip down to New Orleans in 1805, he met Philip Nolan. Nolan was a lively young man who was liable to do things without thinking. Ingham thinks that Burr may have met Nolan at a dinner party. It might have been at Fort Massac in present-day Illinois or, perhaps, some place nearby along the river. Ingham blames the Devil for this meeting. Burr noticed Nolan and spoke to him. He walked with him and even took Nolan on a trip for a day or two on his flatboat. Nolan was held spellbound by Burr. The next year was very dull for Nolan. Burr had given Nolan permission to write to him and he wrote Burr very careful letters, but he used lofty words and pompous language. Burr never answered any of these letters. The other men in the army camp made fun of Nolan because he spent so much time writing to a politician who did not even bother to answer him. The other officers spent their time playing cards. Burr came back. He was not a mere lawyer then. He acted as though he had conquered the country, but he disguised his intentions. He was a very successful lawyer. He had attended many public dinners. Many local newspapers praised Burr. People were saying that Burr had the support of an army and that he would soon rule an empire. Nolan was very happy when Burr arrived. Within an hour after his arrival at the fort where Nolan was stationed, Burr sent for Nolan. Burr asked Nolan to take him out in his flatbottom boat. He said he would like to see a thick growth of sugar cane or, perhaps, a cottonwood tree. He really wanted to lead him astray. When they had finished sailing, Burr had won Nolan over completely to his side. Even though he did not know it, Nolan was from that moment "a man without a country."

Comment

Ingham has described, but not too clearly, the treason of Philip Nolan. Although Nolan is a fictional character, Aaron Burr, the man who causes Nolan's downfall, is a very important historical person.

It must be remembered that, except for New Orleans, the territory in which Nolan was stationed was largely unsettled. The United States bought the Louisiana Territory from France in 1803. Fort Massac, where Burr and Nolan probably met, was just across the Ohio River from the Louisiana Territory, in southernmost Illinois. Illinois was still part of the Indiana Territory at that time. It did not become a state until 1818. In 1805, the year Nolan is supposed to have met Burr for the first time, Burr actually traveled from Pittsburgh to New Orleans. The normal method of travel would be by flatboat down the Ohio and Mississippi Rivers. Suspecting that Burr planned to lead a revolt of the western territories in order to set up an empire, President Jefferson had Burr arrested. He was tried for treason in Richmond, Virginia, but he was found not guilty. The reason was that he was not present when the actual revolt or conspiracy took place. We are not told, but we may suppose that Nolan was present and, therefore, was found guilty.

Burr made the first trip from Pittsburgh to New Orleans in 1805 and he received a great deal of publicity. At that time there was border trouble between the United States and the Spanish territory of Florida. Differences between Spain and the United States were settled that same year and Burr was deprived of any legal excuse to attack the Spanish territories in order to seize land for himself. He made a second trip, this time in August of 1806, and was charged with treason twice in Kentucky and a third time in Richmond, Virginia.

Both Burr and Nolan are described as dashing, but Burr appears in this story primarily as a plotter whose brilliance brings excitement to Nolan. Nolan is leading a dull life in a frontier barracks. Burr seems to have an army to support him and there is talk that he will lead an empire. Nolan on the other hand, is offered card playing as his only excitement. We will later learn that he was used to excitement and adventure as a youth.

NOTES

Aaron Burr (1756–1836) was a soldier in the Revolutionary War and Vice-President of the United States (1801–1805). He had also been Attorney General of New York State (1789) and a United States Senator (1791–1797). He ruined his political career when he killed his old political enemy, Alexander Hamilton (1757–1804) in a duel in Weehawken, New Jersey in 1804. He made his highly publicized trips through the western territories the next two years. He was suspected of plotting to seize some of this territory and establish an empire. He was betrayed by General Wilkinson, a fellow conspirator. After he was found not guilty, he spent the next four years (1808–1812) outside the United States. He tried to get English help for a revolt in Mexico and then attempted to get Napoleon's aid in seizing Spanish territories in North America. He offered to bring about a war between England and the United States to make this possible. When these schemes failed, he returned to the United States in 1812 and he practiced law until his death in 1832.

Orleans or New Orleans was the capital of the newly acquired Louisiana Territory.

Fort Massac was earlier known as Fort Massiac. It had been a French fort (1756–1764), but was abandoned and destroyed by Indians. It was rebuilt by the United States Army in 1794, and kept as a fort until 1814. It was located on the Ohio River on the southernmost part of present-day Illinois.

Monongahela, Sledge, High-Low-Jack, Bourbon, Euchre, and Poker are all card games.

Weekly Arguses: This is a reference to the small-town newspapers of the period. *The Weekly Argus* was a popular name for such papers. Newspapers gave a great deal of publicity to Burr's trips through the western territories.

Seduce means to corrupt or lead someone from his duty or from his right conduct.

Canebrake and Cottonwood Tree: Burr, supposedly, as a New Yorker, would not have been familiar with either sugar cane or the cottonwood tree. In any case, Burr expressed interest in seeing these as an excuse to get Nolan to take him away from the fort so that he could persuade him to join his conspiracy without interference.

NOLAN CURSES THE UNITED STATES

Ingham claims that he did not know what Burr planned to do and says "it is none of our business now." Burr's scheme fell through and President Jefferson set out to break Burr's plans by having him tried for treason at Richmond, Virginia. At the same time, in the Mississippi Valley, the "small fry" in the United States Army who were involved in the conspiracy were tried by military courts for treason. Many colonels and majors in the Army and even the unimportant Lieutenant Nolan were tried. He was sick of the Army and had been willing to betray it. He would have followed any order Aaron Burr gave him. The trials lasted a long time. All the important people ("big flies") escaped. Ingham says that, as far as he knows, it was right that they were not found guilty. Nolan was found guilty. No one would have heard of Nolan, but he lost his temper when asked by the court if he wanted to say anything to prove that he had always been loyal to the United States. He said, "Damn the United States! I wish I may never hear of the United States again!"

Comment

Edward Everett Hale uses heavy **irony** in this paragraph. It is a bitter attack on treason and, to a lesser extent, shows that Hale did not want the United States to be ruled by presidents from a single class or a single section of the country.

Edward IV (1442–1483), the first English king from the House of York, had to defend his newly established throne against his own brother, the Duke of Clarence. Thomas Jefferson, the third President of the United States, faced a similar problem when Burr conspired against the new American republic. Both Burr and Clarence are used in this story as symbols of treachery.

Later in the story, Ingham says he wrote *The Man Without a Country* as a warning to young men who might want to imitate the treason of Philip Nolan or that of either Vallandigham or Tattnall. These two he also considered to be traitors. It is, therefore, clear that Ingham does not mean what he says when he speaks of Burr's treachery or the escape of the important conspirators. Ingham says he does not know what Burr meant to do. This is Hale's ironic, humorous, and bitter way of saying that everyone knows exactly what Burr planned to do. He planned to revolt against the United States. When he says that "it is none of our business" what Burr planned to do, he means that it is definitely our business. When he says that it is perhaps right that the important traitors escaped, this is Hale's ironic way of saying that it is Not right at all that they escaped. The strong stand of Edward Everett Hale against treason becomes even clearer when one recalls that this story was written during the Civil War. Hale was completely opposed to the revolt of the southern states against the Union.

It is part of Hale's humor to treat a serious matter as though it were not serious. He compares the trial of traitors in the United States Army to the production of a play or a show ("spectacle"). He calls the treason trial a "novelty," that is, something new and different. A "novelty" is usually a fad and of no great importance. Hale, of course, regards these trials as very serious things. Four of the first five presidents of the United States were from Virginia and all came from old and wealthy families. They are: George Washington (1789–1797), Thomas Jefferson (1801–1809), James Madison (1809–1817), and James Monroe (1817–1825). John Adams (1797–1801), the 2nd president of the United States, was born in Massachusetts. There is no "House of Virginia." In England a royal family is referred to in this fashion. For example, the present rulers of

England belong to the House of Windsor. The United States is a republic and does not permit royal or noble titles. When Hale has Ingham refer to certain American presidents as the "House of Virginia," he simply means that it is not truly democratic for all presidents to come from the same class or area. Later on, Nolan tells Danforth that he is delighted that Abraham Lincoln, who came from a poor family, is President.

NOTES

Break On A Wheel was the name for a cruel form of execution used for traitors in earlier times. Hale only means "punish" or "crush" when he uses this expression.

Provincial Stage. This old-fashioned expression refers to theaters in small towns and villages. Before the days of the movies, many towns had theaters for the presentation of plays and shows. Traveling companies would visit theaters in the more remote towns, but the acting would not be as good as in large cities like New York, Boston, or Philadelphia.

Courts-Martial are Army or Navy courts which try service men and officers for breaking military rules or committing treason.

WHY NOLAN CURSED THE UNITED STATES

Colonel Morgan was the chief judge at the military trial of Lieutenant Philip Nolan. He was shocked when he heard Nolan curse the United States. Half of the officers assisting Colonel Morgan as judges at the trial had fought in the American

Revolution. They had risked their lives for the United States. In his anger Nolan cursed it in a very silly and arrogant way. To Nolan the United States had little meaning. When he was a boy in the West, there were two plots against the United States, the "Spanish Plot" and the "Orleans Plot." He had been educated on a plantation and the best company there consisted of Spanish officers and French merchants from New Orleans. He did not have much education in a formal sense, but he learned more when he went on a business trip to Vera Cruz, Mexico. One winter his father, if Ingham's memory is correct, hired an Englishman for him as a private teacher. He spent half of his youth hunting horses with an older brother in Texas. Even so, the United States had fed him since he enlisted in the Army and he had sworn his Christian oath to be faithful to the United States. His uniform and his sword were given him by the United States. As a matter of fact, Aaron Burr picked out Nolan only because he had been chosen by the United States as a trustworthy and honorable man. These reasons are given to explain why Nolan damned his country. Ingham does not excuse him, however.

Comment

Ingham explains why Philip Nolan cursed his country and also why he betrayed her. He knew very little about the United States. His early years were spent mostly in the company of foreigners: Spaniards, Frenchmen, Englishmen, and Mexicans. New Orleans at that time was alternately a Spanish and a French possession. Even his hunting trips to Texas took him away from the United States for it was then part of the Spanish province of New Spain. Nevertheless, Nolan promised to support the United States when he enlisted in the Army.

NOTES

Spanish Plot refers to a series of related plots between Spaniards and Americans of the West dating from 1786. Spain hoped to protect her possessions in Florida and Louisiana by encouraging Americans in the West to make themselves independent of the United States. These plots came to an end after the signing of the Pinckney Treaty of 1795. This treaty fixed the boundaries between the United States and West Florida, gave Americans the right to sail the entire Mississippi River, and granted Americans the right to use the Port of New Orleans, which was a Spanish possession.

Orleans Plot: Many American settlers in the West plotted as early as 1802 to attack New Orleans in order to gain control of the Mississippi River. Most American shipping in the West at that time traveled down the Mississippi. There was no need for such a plot after Jefferson bought the whole territory in 1803.

Ark: A large, flat-bottomed boat used on the Mississippi and Ohio Rivers.

COLONEL MORGAN SENTENCES NOLAN

From that day until the day he died, Philip Nolan heard the name of the United States only one time more. He was sentenced that day, September 23, 1807, and he died, almost 56 years later, on May 11, 1863. For the rest of his life he was a man without a country. Colonel Morgan was very shocked. He would not have been more shocked if Nolan had compared George Washington to Benedict Arnold or if Nolan had shouted "God save King George" in the court room. Colonel Morgan took all the members of his court to his private chamber. He returned in fifteen minutes and his face was white as a sheet. He then told Nolan the sentence of the court. Nolan was never to hear the name of the United States again. This sentence had to be approved by the President before it was final.

Comment

In these paragraphs, Hale reveals the sentence imposed upon Nolan, but he does not yet describe the reaction of Nolan. He describes the emotional state of Colonel Morgan. Colonel Morgan is a veteran of the American Revolution and is therefore shocked to hear a man in the uniform of the United States curse his native land. George Washington, our first President, was the Commander-in-Chief of the Continental Army during the Revolutionary War. He was so popular that he received all the electoral votes in the election of 1789. Because of their admiration for him, Americans have called him the "Father of Our Country." Benedict Arnold, on the other hand, was a well-known traitor. He was an outstanding general in the Revolutionary War, but he attempted to betray his own troops to the English in 1780. When his plot failed, he had to flee the country. Colonel Morgan feels that Nolan is as much a traitor as Benedict Arnold. Apparently all the members of Colonel Morgan's court are equally shocked. It took them only fifteen minutes to agree on the verdict. The Colonel is still angry and shocked when he returns to the court room. That is why his face is white.

NOTES

God Save King George would indicate allegiance to England. Englishmen show that they are loyal Englishmen when they say, "God save the King." Americans, on the other hand, show that they are loyal Americans when they salute or pledge allegiance to the flag.

King George: The king of England at the time of Nolan's trial was George III (1760–1820). He was king of England during the American Revolution and the War of 1812. In the Declaration of Independence, mostly written by Thomas Jefferson, the American colonists declared that they were rebelling against the "absolute tyranny" of George III. In Rip Van Winkle, a tale written some 13 years after the trial of Nolan, Rip Van Winkle angers a group of Americans when he says, "I am ... a loyal subject of the king, God bless him!" Rip, however, had been asleep for 20 years and had never heard of the American Revolution.

George Washington (1732–1799) was a member of the Continental Congress when the Revolutionary War broke out in 1775. He was then chosen Commander-in-Chief of the Continental Army. When the war ended in 1783, he retired to his estate at Mount Vernon. He was elected the first President of the United States and served two terms of office.

Benedict Arnold (1741–1801) was an excellent general and a brave soldier in the American Revolution. However, he began to betray his country to the English after he was court-martialed in 1778, as a result of trouble with civilian authorities in the city of Philadelphia. He was given command of West Point in 1780, and he tried to turn over the fort and his army to the English General Andre. His plan failed and he had to flee. He spent the rest of his life in England and Canada.

THE MAN WITHOUT A COUNTRY

TEXTUAL ANALYSIS

PART 2

NOLAN SENT AS A PRISONER TO NEW ORLEANS

Nolan laughs when he hears the sentence. Everyone else remains silent for a whole minute. After that Nolan was not so cocky. Next Colonel Morgan tells the Marshal to take Nolan as a prisoner to New Orleans in an armed boat and to hand him over to the Navy commander there. The Marshal gives his orders to his men and Nolan is lead out of the court room. Then the Colonel tells the Marshal that no one is to mention the United States to Nolan. He asked the Marshal to give his best regards to Lieutenant Michell in New Orleans and to ask that he see that no one mention the United States to Nolan while he is aboard ship. Morgan tells the Marshal that he will receive orders in writing from the officer on duty that evening. He declares the court adjourned.

THE MAN WITHOUT A COUNTRY

Comment

Nolan at first thinks that the sentence is a kind of joke, but soon realizes that no one else thinks it is funny. He laughs because he thinks it is a joke and also because he is proud and does not want to admit to himself that he has been humbled. He also hears Colonel Morgan instruct the Marshal to conduct him as a prisoner to New Orleans and he knows that this is not a joke. Ingham says that Nolan was not to hear the name of the United States but one more time. This one time is when Morgan sentences him "never to hear the name of the United States again."

NOTES

A Marshal is an officer who is in charge of prisoners.

Without Day: This legal phrase is a translation of the Latin sine die. When a court is adjourned without day or sine die, it means that no date has been set for the court to meet again.

Lieutenant Mitchell is a naval officer. It is not yet clear to Nolan that he will spend the rest of his life aboard United States Navy ships in exile.

NOLAN PUT ABOARD THE NAUTILUS

Ingham guesses that Colonel Morgan went to Washington with a record of the court-martial of Nolan and explained the case to President Jefferson. He is certain that President Jefferson approved the sentence. In any case, others have told Ingham that they saw the President's signature on the record of Nolan's trial. Nolan is put aboard the United States Navy ship Nautilus in New Orleans. Before the Nautilus reached the North Atlantic coast of the United States, Jefferson had approved the sentence. From that moment Nolan was certainly a man without a country. A plan for handling Nolan was adopted at the time and followed ever after. They probably got the idea from the fact that Nolan had to be sent by water from Fort Adams to New Orleans. The Secretary of the Navy was asked to put Nolan aboard a ship that was headed on a long cruise. He was asked to see that Nolan was kept aboard ship so it would be certain that he would never see or hear of the United States again. Ingham is not sure who the Secretary of the Navy was at that time. It was probably the first Crowninshield, but he does not remember. There were many long cruises in those days and the government did not generally favor the Navy. Most of what Ingham knows of this story is hearsay, so he is not sure where the Nautilus made its cruise. The commander of the Nautilus, however, set up the rules governing Nolan's imprisonment aboard ship. Those rules were probably followed till the day Nolan died. The commander might have been either Tingey or Shaw. They are now old men. Ingham thinks it was probably a younger man, however.

Comment

Ingham is fairly sure of his information as he describes Nolan's trip down the river to the United States Navy vessel and the President's approval of Nolan's sentence. He is not at all certain about the names of the other men involved at the time. Earlier he had claimed that he had a good memory for names and people. It is amusing to see now how wrong he was. The rules and regulations - "etiquette and the precautions" - governing Nolan's imprisonment will be described later as "mild." He is not locked up, but he is generally restricted to the ship he is attached to.

NOTES

The Nautilus was a ship in the United States Navy at the time. However, Hale only uses the name because it makes his story seem true. The Nautilus was famous for its part in the Barbary War against the North African pirates.

Fort Adams was located in present-day Mississippi, not far from Natchez on the Mississippi River. It was built, in 1798, as an army post to guard the American frontier. It was later abandoned when America acquired Western Florida and the Louisiana Territory. Just before he dies, Nolan will ask Danforth to set up a stone in his memory either at Fort Adams or New Orleans.

Crowninshields. As explained earlier, there were officially two brothers by this name who were named Secretary of the Navy. Ingham cannot remember the first Crowninshield because he never took office.

Tingey: Thomas Tingey (1750–1829) could not possibly have been the commander of the Nautilus in 1807. He was commandant of the Washington Navy Yard from 1804 to his death in 1829, and he never left this post.

Shaw: There were several officers by this name in the Navy in 1807. Perhaps Ingham is thinking of Commander T. Darrah Shaw, but he did not enter the Navy until 1820. There was a Captain John Shaw in the Navy in 1807. In any case, Ingham's memory is bad and Hale does not expect us to discover which Shaw he is thinking of.

Etiquette does not mean merely manners or polite behavior. It means the professional rules or regulations to be followed.

ORIGINAL INSTRUCTIONS FOR HANDLING NOLAN

About 1837, when Ingham was the second officer aboard the Intrepid, he saw an official document which described the rules to be followed in handling Nolan. He has always regretted the fact that he never made a copy of the regulations. However, he lists the rules as he remembers them. The document was written in Washington and must have been dated 1807. The letter is merely addressed to "Sir" and says that a Lieutenant Neale will deliver Philip Nolan, who used to a be lieutenant in the United States Army, to the person addressed. Nolan was tried by a court-martial and said under oath that he hoped he might never hear of the United States again. The court gave him his wish when it sentenced him. The President has asked that the Navy Department carry out this order for the time being. These are the rules: (1) Nolan is to be taken aboard ship and is not to be allowed to escape. (2) He is to be given a cabin ("quarters"), food ("rations"), and clothing that an Army lieutenant would get if he were traveling aboard the ship on government business. (3) The officers of the ship may make Nolan part of their company if they wish. (4) He is not to be insulted in any way. (5) Unless absolutely necessary, no one is to remind him that he is a prisoner. (6) However, he is not to hear of the United States or receive any information or news about it.

Even though Nolan may receive various privileges, officers aboard ship are never to break this rule. Nolan's exact punishment is never to hear of the United States. The government does not want Nolan ever to see the country he disowned. Before the three-year cruise is up, new orders will be issued to carry out the six rules. An official by the name of W. Southard signed this order on behalf of the Secretary of the Navy.

Comment

These regulations governing Nolan's imprisonment appear at this point to be very kind. He is to be a prisoner, but no one is to even mention this unless absolutely necessary. He is to be given all the privileges of an officer and may join other officers in their conversations, meals, and games. The great **irony** of the story is that Nolan is given what he asked for in a fit of temper. Ordinarily it is kind to give a man what he asks for. Nolan, however, will later learn that he does not at all want the thing he asked for. In any case, he never really expected this sentence.

NOTES

W. Southard is a fictional name, but the letter correctly indicates that there was no active Secretary of the Navy in 1807. Jacob Crowninshield never assumed office.

Intrepid: A famous ship by this name was sunk or blown up in Tripoli harbor in 1804, during the Barbary War.

INSTRUCTIONS TRAVEL WITH NOLAN

Ingham regrets that he did not copy down the document in full. If he had, there would be no flaws in the first part of this "sketch." Captain Shaw, or whoever was commander of the Nautilus, would have handed these instructions on to the next commander. They would be given to every commander to whom Nolan was assigned. Ingham believes that this document is today in the possession of the commander of the Levant as his authority for holding Nolan prisoner.

Comment

Ingham is fairly accurate in calling this story a "sketch." That is, the story is, for the most part, about a single character, Philip Nolan. *The Man Without a Country* is a brief composition. In other respects this story is not a "sketch." It presents more than one scene and the plot and the telling of it are complicated. There are several important scenes or incidents. This will be made clear in examining the plot from the point of view of the narrator, Frederic Ingham. He reads an announcement in a newspaper. He thinks about him and then tells the story of Philip Nolan's trial and imprisonment. He attempts to quote the original letter of instructions governing Nolan's imprisonment. He recalls from hearsay three important incidents: (1) Nolan's reading of *The Lay of the Last Minstrel*, (2) the meeting between Mrs. Graff, and Nolan on the Warren, and (3) Nolan's heroism in an encounter with an English ship. Ingham does not meet Nolan until about 1820 or 1822. He then gives an eye-witness account of Nolan's behavior when a slave ship was captured. Nolan and Ingham are separated at the end of that cruise. Ingham then relates two incidents from hearsay: (1) a supposed meeting between Burr and Nolan and (2) Nolan's maps are discussed by Truxton and others. Ingham tells of a conversation aboard the Intrepid when he himself was captain. He tells of writing to Nolan twice a year and of his efforts to free him. To his "sketch" Ingham later attaches a letter by Danforth giving an account of Nolan's last days. Sketches are usually simple in plot and built around one character, one scene, or one incident. *The Man Without a Country* is composed of several scenes and incidents and the plot is complicated.

NOLAN IS AN EMBARRASSMENT TO OTHER OFFICERS

Ingham believes that the rules governing the treatment of Nolan aboard ship, such as the one he was on with Nolan, were the ones originally established on the Nautilus. Officers did not like to have Nolan in their dining room ("mess") because it meant that they could not talk about home, politics, letters from home, or war and peace. These are the subjects of conversations more than half of the time at sea. Everyone thought it was cruel that when he met others, they could not say anything to one another. They could only salute. At last a plan was discovered. He was not allowed to talk to the enlisted men, unless an officer was present. He could talk with officers whenever Nolan or they wanted to. He began to grow shy, but he was fond of some people. Ingham was one of his friends. The captain of the ship would ask Nolan to have dinner with him on Monday night. Each dining room ("mess") aboard ship would take turns inviting him. If the ship was small, Nolan would have dinner in each dining room frequently because there are not many dining rooms aboard a small ship. He always ate his breakfast in his own stateroom. There was always a guard nearby to watch his door. He had breakfast alone. When the marines or sailors had a special party they were permitted to invite Nolan. Nolan would arrive with another officer and the men would not be permitted to talk about home while Nolan was there. There was a theory that the sight of Nolan's punishment gave the enlisted men a good lesson. They called him "Plain Buttons," because he did not wear buttons with the United States initials or coat of arms on them.

Comment

Ingham now describes the effects of Nolan's sentence. It had earlier been described as "mild," but it is really cruel. Nolan becomes lonely, pitiful, and something of a freak. He now begins to learn how important one's country is. He is cut off from a free contact with others because of his sentence. For more than half of the time the men aboard ship talk about home. Nolan had said that he never wanted to hear of the United States again. He becomes a burden to every ship he is on. He is also a living symbol of the result of treachery to one's country. He begins to realize the full **irony** of his sentence. Irony in this case means a difference between what was hoped for and what took place. In his anger, Nolan said he hoped he would never hear of the United States again. When he gets his wish, he finds it is not what he wanted, that it is a terrible thing.

NOTES

Mess here means a group of military men who take their meals together. It also means either the room where meals are served or the meal itself.

Watch: "On the watch" means "on duty." Aboard ship the officers and men are divided into two groups. They take turns, usually for four hours at a time, in running the ship.

Marines are the soldiers of the United States Navy. The Marine Corps, as a division of the Navy was founded in 1798. Small groups of Marines are to be found aboard larger ships of the United States Navy. They usually stand guard by the captain's quarters and other important places aboard ship.

Sentinel: This is a person who guards or watches. Aboard ship he might be either a sailor or a marine.

Insignia: A mark or emblem. In this case the emblem referred to is either the American eagle or the initials "U.S.A."

Stateroom is the private sleeping quarters of an officer aboard ship. We will learn later that no one else ever enters Nolan's stateroom.

CENSORSHIP OF NOLAN'S READING AND THE LAY OF THE LAST MINSTREL

Ingham recalls that shortly after he joined the Navy, he visited Egypt in company with some older officers from his own ship and also from the Brandywine. They met the officers from the Brandywine in Alexandria, Egypt. The two groups got together and made a trip to Cairo and the Pyramids. They traveled by donkey. Some of the older officers began to talk about Nolan. They told about the rules governing Nolan's reading. Nolan had a lot of time to kill, because he was almost never permitted to go ashore, even if the ship was in port for months. For that reason everyone was allowed to lend him books. However, the books could not have been published in America or make any reference to the United States. It was not difficult to find such books at that time. In Europe few people then talked very much about the United States. Nolan read almost all the foreign newspapers aboard ship, but somebody had to cut out advertisements or occasional paragraphs that referred to the United States. Unfortunately, when they did that, they would have to cut out something harmless from a news item on the other side of the page. Therefore, Nolan would find paragraphs cut out of accounts of Napoleon's battles or a speech by Canning because the opposite side of the page had an advertisement for a ship sailing to New York or a part of a speech by the President of the United States. This is the first time Ingham heard about the rules governing. Nolan's reading. Later on Ingham had a lot to do with Nolan's reading.

Phillips, an officer who was also on the trip to Cairo and the Pyramids, then told a story about something that happened at the Cape of Good Hope when Nolan was on his first cruise. Ingham never learned anything else about this cruise. When the Nautilus arrived in this British colony, the officers visited the English Admiral and the British fleet. It was the polite thing to do. Because the Nautilus was going on a voyage in the Indian Ocean, Phillips borrowed many books from an English officer, among them *The Lay of the Last Minstrel*. This was an unexpected bit of good luck. All the American officers had heard of this book, but few had seen it. It had not been published very long. No one thought it likely that there would be any reference to the United States in that book. However, Phillips, said that Shaw once cut out *The Tempest* from the works of William Shakespeare, before he would let Nolan have the volume. Shaw said that the Bermudas, which are mentioned in the play, should belong to the United States and one day the United States would own them.

Nolan was allowed to join a group of officers on deck one afternoon. They were smoking and reading aloud. It is not customary to do this now, but when Ingham was young it was a popular way to spend time. Nolan read aloud to the others when it came his turn. He read very well. No one in that group had ever read the book before. They only knew that the book was filed with magic, told a story about knights on the Scottish-English border, and that it took place a long, long, time ago. Nolan read for a time then stopped to drink something and then began again without knowing what he was to read next. He began reading the lines:

Breathes there the man, with soul so dead, Who never to himself hath said -

(Is there a living man so lacking in feeling that he has never said-)

Comment

This is one of the most important incidents in the story. It is ironic, dramatic, highly allusive, and furnishes the title of the story. **Allusions** are brief, but often important references. They refer to people, events, places, books, etc. In this section Ingham refers to *The Tempest* by Shakespeare, *The Lay of the Last Minstrel* by Scott, the poetry of Hesiod, and speeches by Canning and presidents of the United States. Hale has a special reason for making **allusions** to the works of Shakespeare, Hesiod, and Scott.

There are two reasons for the **allusion** to *The Tempest*. First of all it shows how fiercely Nolan's reading was censored. Shaw does not permit Nolan to read this play of Shakespeare because there is a reference to some islands which Shaw feels that United States should own. The second reason is ironic. Shaw thinks that the only harmful thing is the reference to Bermuda ("Bermoothes"), but Hale most likely chose this reference to *The Tempest*, because it tells a story of treason and exile. If Nolan read this play, he would see that he was much like the evil Antonio who rebelled against his own brother Prospero. He took from him the throne of the dukedom of Milan. He could also compare himself to Prospero who is set adrift on the ocean and is cast up on a lonely isle.

Hale is also ironic when he has Ingham refer to the poetry of Hesiod as "innocent" or harmless. It is true that the poetry of Hesiod would be "innocent" in that there are no references to the United States in his poetry. It would not violate the rules governing Nolan's reading. In another sense, however, it would wound or harm Nolan to read Hesiod's Works and Days. Hesiod relates that his own brother Perses betrayed him and left the land of his birth. Hesiod pleads with his brother to return home and make peace with him. Unlike Perses, Nolan cannot return home and Hesiod's poetry would hurt Nolan by reminding him of his own treason and exile. The **irony** is this: Ingham is sincere when he says that Hesiod is "innocent," but the reader who knows Hesiod is aware that Nolan would be hurt in a deeper way in reading it.

Ingham is not aware of the **irony** of his reference to *The Tempest* or to the poetry of Hesiod. He would be quite aware of the **irony** of Nolan reading *The Lay of the Last Minstrel*. **Irony** here simply means that the exact opposite of what was expected takes place. Because the story takes place in 16th-century Scotland and relates very distant and romantic things, Nolan and the other officers were not prepared for the passage that Nolan happened to read. It was harmless, because it did not violate the censorship rules. It is harmful in another way. The section of the poem which Nolan reads aloud contains a description of a man without a country. Nolan, in other words, finds himself reading aloud to a group of officers a section of a poem which really describes himself. He is so hurt inside that he has trouble reading, he turns pale, then blushes, and finally, as described below, he throws *The Lay of the Last Minstrel* into the ocean.

| NOTES

The Brandywine was a United States frigate in service between 1819 and 1826.

Cairo and the Pyramids: Cairo, the capital of Egypt, is located on the Nile River some distance from the Mediterranean. The Pyramids are not far from Cairo.

Alexandria is the sea port of Egypt and is located near one of the many mouths of the Nile.

Dons is an old-fashioned term, according to Ingham. This indicates that he is an older man. He says the term is no longer used. Don is a Spanish word and is used in speaking of important people or gentlemen. The older officers were once called "Dons."

Hesiod was a Greek poet of the 8th century before Christ. He is known as the author of three works: *Works and Days*, *Theogony*, and *Catalogue of Women*.

Napoleon or Napoleon Bonaparte (1769–1821) was Emperor of France (1804–1814) and a great general. He fought Austria, Prussia, England, Russia, and many other countries and created a large French Empire in Europe. He was forced to give up his throne after he was defeated at Leipzig in 1814. He returned from exile on the island of Elba in 1815 and was finally defeated at the Battle of Waterloo the same year. He spent the last years of his life in exile on the Island of Saint Helena. Naturally, Nolan would be interested in reading about Napoleon's battles. Napoleon sold the Louisiana Territory to the United States in 1803.

Canning: George Canning (1770–1827) was a famous English statesman and orator.

Packet: A sailing vessel or steamship which used to carry mail, passengers, and freight at regularly scheduled times.

President's Message: It is customary for the President of the United States to send an annual message to Congress on the State of the Union. There were eleven presidents of the United States during Nolan's 56 years of imprisonment.

The Lay Of The Last Minstrel was written by Sir Walter Scott, a Scots poet, and published in 1805, two years before Nolan's sentence. The incident took place while Nolan was on his first voyage. That would be between 1807 and 1810. Scott's poem is divided into six parts called "cantos." It appears that each of the officers read one canto and then passed the book along to another officer. Ingham would then be the sixth person to read since he began to read the sixth canto.

Shaw: Ingham now seems certain that Shaw was commander of the Nautilus.

The Tempest of William Shakespeare was written about 1611. The play tells the story of the exile of Prospero and his daughter Miranda on a lonely island. The reference to Bermuda or Bermoothes is found in Act I, scene two:

Safely in harbor

Is the king's ship; in the deep nooks, where once Though call'dst me up at midnight, to fetch dew From the still-vexed Bermoothes, there she's hid.

The Bermudas are a group of islands about 650 miles southeast of North Carolina. They were originally called the

Bermudez after Juan de Bermudes who discovered them. They are now a British crown colony and generally referred to simply as Bermuda.

By Jove is an old-fashioned way of saying "By God."

Border Chivalry: The border referred to is the one between England and Scotland. For centuries there was warfare or raids carried on between the chivalry or warriors on horseback of Scotland and England.

Ten Thousand Years Ago is an exaggeration. Ingham simply means a long time ago. The story related in Scott's poem actually takes place in the 16th century.

NOLAN THROWS THE LAY OF THE LAST MINSTREL INTO THE OCEAN

This was the first time any of these officers ever heard Scott's poem. Nolan continued to read. He next read, without thinking:

This is my own, my native land!

(This is my own country; this is my native land!)

Everyone then realizes that it is going to be difficult for Nolan, but he expected to finish, it seems. He turns pale and then begins to read again.

Whose heart hath ne'er within him burned, As home his footsteps he hath turned From wandering on a foreign strand? - If such there breathe, go, mark him well.

(Who has never felt very much excited when he started out for home from a foreign country? - If there is such a person, notice him carefully.)

At this point the other officers feel nervous and hope that Nolan might, some way, skip two pages. Nolan was too confused to think of that. He choked a bit, blushed, and then read:

For him no minstrel raptures swell; High though his titles, proud his name. Boundless his wealth as wish can claim; Despite these titles, power, and pelf, The wretch, concentered all in self. . . .

(Poems or songs do not excite such a person; even though he may have very important titles, an old and honored family name, the unhappy person who thinks only of himself ...)

Nolan's voice choked at this point and he could not read any more. He got up and threw the book into the ocean. He then went to his cabin. Phillips said that no one saw him for two months. Phillips had to make a feeble excuse to the English doctor who had lent him *The Lay of the Last Minstrel.*

Comment

It is by accident that Nolan read the canto of Scoth's poem which describes and ridicules a man who is very much like himself. Nolan and the officers who are listening to him are aware that the man described in the poem is like Nolan. That is why they are nervous and why Nolan becomes embarrassed and is finally unable to finish reading. Nolan has a quick temper. He was given his unusual sentence because he lost his temper in the court room and cursed the United States. Now he loses his temper again, because what he reads forces him to see himself exactly as others see him. Everyone knows that he is a man without a country.

The man without a country in Scott's poem is lonely, without ordinary human feelings, and he is very selfish. Scott says that anyone who does not have any feeling of love for his native land is an unhappy and miserable person. Such a man does not have these feelings, because he is a selfish person who thinks only of himself. Without love of native land, even wealth and honor cannot make a man happy.

When Nolan finds that he cannot read more, he has time to look ahead at the next four lines. These lines are even worse than the lines he has already read.

Living, shall forfeit fair renown, And doubly dying, shall go down To the vile dust, from when he sprung, Unwept, unhonored, and unsung.

(While he lives, such a man cannot have a good reputation. And when he dies his name and reputation will die with him. When his body rots and becomes dust again, his name and reputation will also die. No one will weep over him, honor him, or sing about him.)

Nolan sees himself described in those lines. His name too will die with him. No one will remember him or honor him, because he is a man without a country. Later on we will learn that Nolan's last request will be for the erection of a stone at either Fort Adams or New Orleans so that he will not be "unwept, unhonour'd, and unsung."

NOTES

Strand means "beach" or "shore."

Mark Him Well means "notice him carefully."

Minstrel is a wandering musician and singer. In the Middle Ages, minstrels used to travel about the county and stop at castles, the homes of rich farmers, and even on the streets to play and sing songs for money. Minstrel often is used to mean "poet."

Raptures are expressions of very great delight. A minstrel or poet expresses his delight in a song or poem. Raptures here means "poems" or "songs."

Pelf means "wealth" or "money." The word usually suggests that the money was not acquired honestly.

Surgeon is a doctor whose specialty is operating. A physician, on the other hand, is a general practitioner. In the Navy at this time, however, all doctors were usually called surgeons.

THE MAN WITHOUT A COUNTRY

TEXTUAL ANALYSIS

PART 3

NOLAN BREAKS DOWN

Phillips' story indicates that about this time Nolan lost his habit of acting very proud and boasting. They say that when Nolan was first imprisoned he took the whole thing as a kind of a joke. He acted as though it did not bother him in the least to be imprisoned aboard ship. He pretended that he liked the sea voyage. However, Phillips says that when Nolan came out of his stateroom two months later, he was an entirely different man. He would no longer take his turn reading aloud with a group of officers unless he knew the book very well. He knew the Bible very well and also the works of Shakespeare. He never became too friendly with other young men after that. When Ingham met Nolan, he was shy. Except for a few friends, Nolan would speak to people only when they spoke to him first. Sometimes he acted as though he was happy, but most of the time he looked nervous and tired. He was like a man whose heart was broken. One time, however, when he was an old man, Ingham heard Nolan speak with great excitement about something in a sermon by Flechier.

Comment

If this story were told in strict chronological order, this would be the **climax** or high point of the story. However, we learn later about events that happened earlier in Nolan's life. This section, nevertheless, clearly marks the two periods in Nolan's life and the great change in his character. Up to this point Nolan has a lot of self-confidence, boasts, is cheerful, hopeful, likes company, and talks a great deal. After the **episode** of *The Lay of the Last Minstrel*, when he finally comes out of his stateroom after hiding there for two months, he is always shy, unsure of himself, despondent and unhappy. Later on we will learn that he also changes his attitude towards his native land.

NOTES

Braggadocio means to boast openly or to brag about one's self, either exaggerating or telling lies. Braggadocio is also the name of a character in *The Faerie Queene* by Edmund Spenser (1552–1599).

Farce is a situation or action that is ridiculous or silly.

Shakespeare: Nolan has the complete works of Shakespeare, except for *The Tempest*. Captain Shaw had that torn out of Nolan's volume of Shakespeare's plays.

Flechier: Esprit Flechier (1632–1710) was a French bishop who gave sermons at the court of Louis XIV of France.

NOLAN'S SECOND CRUISE

When Captain Shaw returns home, everyone is surprised when the ship sails to the Windward Islands and anchors offshore for about one week. The enlisted men think that the officers are tired of eating salted meat and want to have some turtle soup before they return home. However, after several days, the Warren comes to the same meeting-place and the two ships signal one another. The Warren sends letters and papers to Phillips and the other men who were on their way home. Nolan is sent by boat to the Warren together with all possessions. The Warren then sails further away from the United States, probably towards the Mediterranean. This is the beginning of his second cruise. He can tell by the positions of the stars in the sky that the Nautilus is on her way home. He has a look of surprise when he is told that he is to be transferred to the Warren. This transfer to the Warren is a sure sign that Nolan is never going to go home, not even to be put in prison in the United States. Before this, Nolan had probably not thought that his exile from the United States was to be permanent. Altogether he is transferred about 20 times. He spends the rest of his life aboard some of the best ships of the Navy. He never gets closer than 100 miles of the United States.

Comment

Nolan did not fully understand his sentence at first. With his transfer to the Warren, just as the Nautilus is going home, Nolan is given his first hint that he will never see his native land again. In order to make this section mysterious, Hale has Ingham tell of the transfer from the point of view of the enlisted men. They do not know the sailing instructions given the captain. The officers would know, of course, that a meeting has already been arranged between the Warren and the Nautilus. Nolan cannot remain aboard the Nautilus, because it is returning home. Whenever a ship to which Nolan is attached is about to return home, Nolan will have to be transferred to another ship that is either on a cruise or sailing away from the United States. Nolan has already lost his confidence and cockiness. The blank expression on his face indicates both disappointment and surprise. He is suddenly aware of the fact that there is a plan to keep him away from the United States.

NOTES

Captain Shaw. Ingham is still not sure that Shaw was the commander of the Nautilus. Since the incident took place over 50 years before, it is not surprising that he cannot be sure.

Windward Islands. These islands form a chain which stretches from Puerto Rico in the Caribbean Sea to Venezuela in South America. The important Windward Islands are Guadalupe, Dominic, Martinique, St. Lucia, St. Vincent, the Barbados, and Grenada. Large turtles suitable for making turtle soup are found around these islands.

Salt-Junk is salted meat. As there was no refrigeration at this time, ships carried salted meat in barrels. Fresh meat was available only after reaching a port.

Rendez-vous is a French expression which means a planned meeting at a certain time and place.

Outward is naval language means away from the home port of a ship.

Signs Of The Sky means the positions of the stars in the sky. By examining the positions of the stars, sailors can tell in what part of the world they are at a given time.

NOLAN INVITED TO A DANCE

It was perhaps on the Warren, Nolan's second cruise, that Nolan danced with Mrs. Graff. She was then a famous and beautiful woman from the South. The ship had been at anchor in the Bay of Naples for some time and the American officers were very friendly with the officers of the English Navy. The English had many celebrations so the American officers thought that they should give a dance aboard their ship. Ingham cannot figure out how they were able to find room aboard the Warren for a dance for it was a small ship. The ladies wanted to use Nolan's room and felt that they must then ask him to the dance. The captain of the Warren said that they could ask Nolan, but they had to promise not to let him talk to people who might give him news from home. The dance was very successful. They always are on a warship. The women in the family of the American consul were at the dance and probably one or two tourists who were visiting Naples. There were also a number of attractive English girls and married women. Lady Hamilton might have been there.

Comment

The mood of the story changes somewhat for a moment as Ingham begins to tell about the incident that took place on the Warren. Ingham had not yet enlisted in the Navy so he is only telling what others told him. For that reason he cannot be sure of all his facts. Nolan is invited to the dance only because the women have not used his stateroom as a powder room. The dance is a very happy affair at first. It seems that Nolan is also going to break out of his loneliness and enjoy himself in the company of many attractive women. To add to the feminine and happy atmosphere, Hale has Ingham complain humorously about the way women dress. When this story was written women wore hoop-skirts and they took up a lot of room. The ship appears to be crowded with women.

CHARACTER ANALYSIS

Mrs. Graff is a beautiful woman, she has a strong character, and she is patriotic. She apparently approves of Nolan's sentence. She lets Shubrick know that Nolan is safe with her. She reminds Nolan of his treason. Although she is a fictional character, Hale chose the name "Graff," because the Graffs were a prominent family in Philadelphia at the time.

Lady Hamilton is a real person, but she could not have been at the ball. Lady Emma Hamilton (1761–1815) was the wife of Sir William Hamilton (1730–1803), the English ambassador to Naples. She was also the mistress of Lord Nelson (1758–1805), a famous English naval hero. She had been very prominent in the society of Naples, but she returned to England with her husband and Lord Nelson in 1800.

NOLAN'S GUARDS RELAX

The American officers take turns standing by Nolan to see that no one else speaks to him. The dancing is very lively and after a while the officers feel that nothing awkward or embarrassing is going to happen. Something strange happens, however, when one of the English women asks the band to play some American dances. The Negro musicians are happy to do that, but they must first get together to decide what dances are American. They decide to play a set of three dances called the "Virginia Reel," "Money-Musk," and "The Old Thirteen." Dick, who is the leader of the band, announces and the band plays the first two. However, just as he is about to announce. "The Old Thirteen," the captain's special attendant taps Dick on the shoulder and whispers something to him. Dick then merely bows and the musicians begin to play "The Old Thirteen." The American officers teach the English girls how to do this dance. They do not tell them why the dance does not have a name.

Comment

Nolan's presence at the dance seems very awkward at first, but after a while everyone feels relaxed. No one can entirely forget his presence, however. The name of one dance, referring to the original thirteen states, cannot be announced because he is there. There are two contrasting scenes in this paragraph. To one side is Nolan surrounded by officers who are guarding him to see that no one talks to him about America. The larger scene is one of officers and girls enjoying themselves very much as a band of Negro musicians plays for them. This contrast emphasizes the loneliness of Nolan. The English guests are told nothing about Nolan and are not aware that he is a prisoner.

NOTES

Contretemps is a French word which means an awkward or embarrassing accident. It would be awkward or embarrassing if someone were to try to talk about America in Nolan's presence.

American Dances at that time came largely from England and Scotland, so it would be hard to decide which dances were distinctly American. That is why Dick and the other musicians have to figure out which ones to play. Apparently Nolan does not hear the lady ask for "American dances." He is not even supposed to hear the name.

The Old Thirteen cannot be announced because it refers to the 13 original states. It is the third in a set or group of three dances. That is why the captain's orderly is able to stop Dick from announcing it. He knows it must follow the "Virginia Reel" and "Money-Musk."

Dick, the leader of a band of Negro musicians aboard the Warren, is not well educated. That is why he says "Virginny Reel" instead of "Virginia Reel," and "gentlemen and ladies" instead of "ladies and gentlemen." Even at this early time, Negro bands were very popular in the United States.

NOLAN LEFT ALONE ON THE DANCE FLOOR

Ingham now tells the story he meant to tell in the first place. Everyone is now so relaxed that it seems perfectly safe for Nolan to bow and speak to Mrs. Graff. He calls her Miss Rutledge and asks if she remembers him and if she will dance with him. Nolan does all this so fast that Shubrick, the man who is guarding him at that moment, cannot stop him. Mrs. Graff laughs and says that she is now married and that her name is Mrs. Graff. She makes a sign to Shubrick to let him know that she will watch Nolan. Nolan now feels that he has a chance to talk about America and get news from home. He had known Mrs. Graff in Philadelphia and had met her in other places also. It is not possible for Mrs. Graff and Nolan to have a conversation while doing contradances but it is possible to talk while doing the cotillion. He talks to her about her travels, Europe, Mount Vesuvius, and the French. When there is a long space for talk at the end of a set of dances, he turns pale and asks Mrs. Graff what she has heard from home. She, however, reminds Nolan that he once asked never to hear of home again. She leaves him standing alone on the dance floor and walks over to where her husband is standing. Nolan does not dance again.

Comment

When Nolan sees Mrs. Graff, a woman he once knew at home, he hurriedly escapes from Shubrick with the intention of getting news from home from her. He is very much mistaken, however. Mrs. Graff lets Shubrick know that she will watch Nolan and when he tries to talk of home she reminds him of his sentence. For a short while it appeared that Nolan was going to enjoy himself and have hope. When she leaves him alone on the dance floor, he appears more lonely than ever. He does not dance again that night because of her reply. It seems that he never danced again for the rest of his life. When Ingham meets Nolan several years later, no one is permitted to enter Nolan's stateroom. It is likely that Nolan began to enforce that rule after his encounter with Mrs. Graff.

NOTES

Miss Rutledge is the maiden name of Mrs. Graff. Hale chose "Rutledge" as her name before she married, because it is the name of a very important family in Charleston, South Carolina. One member of that family, Edward Rutledge (1749–1800), signed the Declaration of Independence. South Carolina is, of course, a Southern state and Miss Graff is called a "celebrated Southern beauty."

Shubrick. He is unable to act quickly enough to stop Nolan from dancing with Mrs. Graff.

Contradance resembles a square dance. Since partners are frequently exchanged and partners are never beside one another for a long time, it is hard to talk while doing this dance which is also called contredanse or country-dance.

Cotillions are dances where partners are frequently exchanged, but since few people take part in the dance, conversation is possible.

Vesuvius is a volcanic mountain near the Bay of Naples and a famous tourist attraction.

French. At this time Napoleon was still Emperor of the French. Nolan and Mrs. Graff would probably talk about Napoleon's battles.

Bottom Of The Set means the last in a group of dances.

NOLAN PROVES HIS COURAGE IN A FRIGATE-DUEL

Ingham says that he is not telling Nolan's story in proper order. No one can do that. He does tell the stories that have been handed down. He does not tell any stories that have been handed down. He does not tell any stories that he believes to be false. There are many false stories about Nolan. Some people, for example, used to say that Nolan was the "man in the iron mask" and George Pons believed to the day he died that Nolan was the writer, "Junius." He believed that Jefferson imprisoned Nolan for making a dishonest attack on him in print. Ingham now tells a happy story about Nolan. It took place during the War of 1812. He has heard three or four versions of this story, but it is possible that they are really separate events. He does not know the name of the ship on which this **episode** took place.

In any case, when an American frigate was fighting an English frigate at sea, a cannon ball killed a gunnery officer and almost all his men. Nolan appears just as the surgeon and the survivors are taking away the bodies. He holds a ramrod in his hand and he takes command of the gun. He orders some of his men to take the wounded to safety. He is cheerful and for that reason the men have trust in him. He loads the gun, aims it, and orders the men to fire it. He keeps up the men's courage, shows them better ways to handle the heavy shots, and he even makes those who have no experience at sea battles laugh at their own mistakes. The gun he commands fires twice as often as the other guns aboard ship. The captain of the ship comes up to encourage his men. Nolan salutes him and tells him that he is showing the men how guns are fired in the Army artillery.

Comment

Although there are many conflicting and untrue stories about Nolan, Ingham does his best to tell only those that are true. He proves his honesty when he admits that he is not sure of names of certain facts. The event he relates took place during the War of 1812. Nolan shows that he is a very skilled gunnery officer and that he also is concerned about his country. He is brave and risks his life when he comes out of his stateroom and exposes himself to enemy fire. This story and others that Ingham will relate show that Nolan's character has changed. From this point on, Nolan shows that he is devoted to his country. Ingham says he is not sure of the name of the ship and he does not name the officer in command. On his deathbed, however, Nolan tells Danforth the true story of the frigate-duel in which the Java was taken. The Java, an English ship, was taken by Captain William Bainbridge of the American ship Constitution on December 12, 1812.

NOTES

Traditions here are true stories told about Nolan. They are not written stories, but have been passed around by word of mouth.

Myths are stories that are not true. Originally a myth was a story about the pagan gods.

Legion means a very great number.

Man In The Iron Mask was a real person in the time of Louis XIV of France. He was kept in prison and wore a mask covered with black velvet. His real name was perhaps Count Mattioli, but some say he was really the twin brother of Louis XIV or one of Louis' illegitimate sons. Alexandre Dumas wrote a story about him called *The Man in the Iron Mask*. Nolan could not be the "man in the iron mask" because that prisoner died in 1703. In any case, a prisoner of the King of France would not be kept on an American ship. This is an example of the myths or lies told about Nolan.

George Pons is one of those people who believe the myths about Nolan. Pons does not really know who "Junius" was.

Junius is the unknown author of the Letters of Junius. In these letters, which appeared from 1769 to 1771, "Junius" made fun of the government of England at that time. He did not attack Jefferson. Later on many people in England and America used the same name when they wrote attacks on important politicians. For example, someone who called himself "Junius Philaenus" attacked Jefferson in a public letter in 1802. George Pons, according to Ingham, did not know much about history. He should have known that no one by the name of Junius was imprisoned by Jefferson.

War Of 1812. Ingham calls this war between England and America simply "the War."

Frigate-Duels are sea battles between frigates or warships. Many such sea battles took place between English and American ships during the War of 1812. The most famous frigate-duel of the war was between the American Constitution and the English Guerriere in 1812. Captain Isaac Hull defeated the English ship in 30 minutes. Because she proved herself so strong in that fight, the Constitution was nick-named "Old Ironsides." Oliver Wendell Holmes wrote a poem by that name in 1830 when plans were made to dismantle her. The Constitution is still preserved as a national monument.

Ports Square. Ports are openings or windows on a ship. When Ingham says that "a round shot ... entered one of our ports square," he means that a cannon ball was shot directly into the opening where the gun crew was located.

Rammer is a pole used to push the ammunition into place before firing a cannon. It is also called a ramrod.

Cockpit is an apartment below the waterline of a ship where the wounded used to be cared for during a sea battle.

Captain Of That Gun. The man in charge of a cannon or other large gun is called a captain of the gun or a gun captain.

Enemy Struck. In order to indicate willingness to surrender, a ship lowers or "strikes" its flag.

Raw Hands are seamen who lack either experience in battle or experience at sea.

Artillery is a division of the Army which is equipped with guns larger than the ordinary rifle. Nolan was a gunnery or artillery officer in the Army. He, therefore, knows a great deal about guns.

THE COMMODORE GIVES NOLAN HIS SWORD

All the stories about Nolan agree that the following took place. The Commodore thanks Nolan and tells him that neither he nor Nolan will ever forget what happened that day. After the fight, the captain of the English ship (Java) gives his sword to the Commodore as a sign of surrender on the quarter-deck of the American frigate. The Commodore then sends for Nolan and thanks him. He says he will mention Nolan in the official report of the battle. The Commodore then gives Nolan his own dress sword. A man who saw this told Ingham about it. Nolan cries like a baby, because he has not worn a sword since the day he was sentenced at Fort Adams. Nolan always wore the sword the Commodore gave him whenever he took part in public ceremonies. The Commodore does mention Nolan in his report. They say he also asked for a pardon for Nolan. He even wrote a special letter to the Secretary of War, but that did not work. It was about this time that officials in Washington began to ignore Nolan's existence. From then on Nolan remained a prisoner, because no one in Washington would issue an order to release him.

Comment

Because of Nolan's bravery during the War of 1812, a Commodore tries to get a pardon for him. However, no one in Washington pays any attention to Nolan. He remains a prisoner for the rest of his life simply because no official in the Navy Department is interested enough to obtain an order for his release. Nolan has proved himself a loyal American and he has earned a pardon. But the bureaucrats in Washington do not care. When he was sentenced, Nolan acted in a silly and proud manner. Later he became shy and lonely because he saw how cut off from everyone he was. He cries now because for the first time since his imprisonment someone is especially kind to him and praises him. He is a freak aboard ship because he is an Army officer who wears no insignia and carries no sword. His sword would have been taken away from him permanently when he was convicted of treason. For the first time in years now, he can now wear a sword. He looks more like the Army lieutenant that he used to be.

NOTES

Legends are, in this case, stories, supposed to be true, which are handed down by word of mouth.

Commodore is a rank in the United States Navy just below rear admiral and above captain.

William Bainbridge (1774–1833) was in command of the Constitution when it fought the Java. This is the man who Ingham refers to as the Commodore. He was a captain, however.

Captain in the Navy may mean either the man in command of a ship or a man with the rank of captain. This rank is just below commodore and above commander.

Englishman's Sword. Military officers give their swords to the enemy as a sign that they have surrendered. After a sea battle, the surrender ceremony takes place on the quarter-deck.

Quarter-Deck. This is the upper deck to the rear of a ship. It is reserved for officers.

NOLAN AND NUKU-HIVA

Ingham also heard that Nolan was with "Essex" Porter when he seized the Nuku-Hiva ("Nuka-Hiwa") Islands. Ingham is talking about old Porter, not his son. Nolan should have been given command of those islands together with Gamble. Nolan had experience with the army artillery in the West. He knew about fortifications. He had worked very hard on the battery. If Nolan had been left there, that would have solved the question of his punishment. America could also have kept these islands as a watering-station in the Pacific. But Madison and the Virginians gave it away.

Comment

This paragraph offers what might have been a solution for Nolan's unjustly prolonged imprisonment. His knowledge would have been useful. He could have directed the building of a fort on Nuku-Hiva. This paragraph, however, is a digression. The real subject is the territorial expansion of the United States. Captain David Porter seized these islands in the War of 1812 and used them as a rest camp and supply depot for a short time. When Hale wrote this story, America had no possessions in the Pacific. We did not acquire Hawaii until 1898. European powers were seizing islands in the Pacific, especially to use as ports for their ships, but Madison, who was President at the time, did not want further expansion. Ingham, as an old naval officer, would be especially interested in stations for American ships in the Pacific.

NOTES

Old Porter that Ingham speaks of is Captain David Porter (1780–1843). He fought in the war against the pirates of Tripoli and in the War of 1812. He is called "Essex" Porter because he was commander of the Essex during the War of 1812 and he captured nine ships in a very short time. He sailed around Cape Horn into the Pacific in 1812 and then took control for a short time of the Nuku-Hiva Islands. He named the main island Madison Island. There is no doubt that Nolan knew "old Porter," for he asks about "dear Old David Porter" on his death bed. David Dixon Porter (1813–1891) was the son of "Old Porter" and a famous naval officer during the Civil War.

Nukahiwa Islands. The name is usually spelled Nuka-Hiva or Nuku-Hiva. They are part of the French Marquesas Islands in the South Pacific. When America did not remain in control of these islands, the French took possession of them.

Gamble. There are several officers by this name who fought in the War of 1812.

Embrasures are walls built with a place for a gun to fire.

Ravelins are V-shaped fortifications. They point in the direction of the enemy.

Stockades are fences made of posts to surround an area.

French Friends is another example of Ingham's **irony**. France helped America win her independence from England, but serious difficulties arouse later between the two countries. Ingham does not mean that the French are friends. They are enemies.

Watering Place: Naval vessels must, of course, carry fresh water and any place where they can stop to get fresh water is called a watering place.

James Madison was President during the War of 1812. He was born in Virginia.

Virginians: Presidents Washington, Jefferson, Madison, and Monroe were born in Virginia. Ingham and Nolan have both complained that too many presidents have come from Virginia. Ingham is also dissatisfied because Jefferson, Madison, and Monroe were not anxious to expand the territorial limits of the United States.

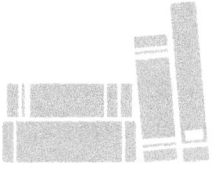

THE MAN WITHOUT A COUNTRY

TEXTUAL ANALYSIS

PART 4

HOW NOLAN SPENT HIS TIME

Ingham thinks Nolan was thirty years old when he was with Porter. Then he must have been about age 80 when he died. When he was 40 he looked as though he was 60. After that however he never seemed to get older. He must have been on every ocean, but hardly ever on land. He must have met more officers than any living man. Nolan once told Ingham that his life was extremely methodical. He used to read five hours a day. He spent two hours working on his scrapbooks and notebooks. In his notebooks he would write notes on what he had read. He had between six and eight scrapbooks. One was used for history, another for natural science, and another for "Odds and Ends." They were filled with bits of plants, ribbons, shells, bone, and wood. He drew well and his drawings in his scrapbooks were both amusing and sad. He spent another two hours devoted to natural history. He called this his pastime. He had birds and fish that the men brought to him. He also had centipedes, cockroaches, and the like. He knew more about houseflies and mosquitoes than any other naturalist.

Others can identify the Lepidoptera and the Steptopotera, however they cannot tell you how to get rid of them or explain why you can never hit them. Even Linnaeus did not know more about that than an idiot. Nolan also walked about and climbed the rigging of the ship. He always exercised and was never ill. He was a good nurse to the men and knew more than many doctors. He was always ready to read prayers to the sick or for the dead or for any other occasion. He read very well.

Comment

Ingham describes Nolan now as a kind and religious man who had learned a great deal. He believes in work, study, and exercise. Nolan is especially interested in science. His life is completely organized. This indicates that, though he has given up hope of freedom, he has not become discouraged. Ingham's attacks on some scientists is not serious. He is only joking. The fact that Nolan looked like a man of 60 when he was only 40 indicates that the first years of his imprisonment were very hard for him. The fact that he never appeared to age during the last 40 years of his life indicates that he was always in good health and that he had learned to accept his imprisonment.

NOTES

Formal, as used when Ingham says that Nolan knew many officers in a "formal way," means that he had met them but was never very friendly with them.

Iron Mask: Nolan knows that he is called the "iron mask." Like the "man in the iron mask," Nolan carefully organized his time so that he would not become soft or insane in prison.

Natural Science is any science, like biology, chemistry, or physics, that deals with the physical universe.

Natural History is biology.

Naturalist is a zoologist or a botanist. He studies either plants or animals or both.

Lepidoptera is the scientific name for moths and butterflies. It means "scaley wing."

Steptopotera. Hale appears to have invented this word. It should, in any case, be spelled steptoptera and it means "crowned wing."

Linnaeus is the Latin name of the great Swedish naturalist and doctor, Carl Von Linne (1707-1778). He is famous for his classification of plants.

John Foy is no one in particular. Here it means any idiot.

CAPTURE OF A SLAVE SHIP

Ingham first became acquainted with Nolan about six or eight years after the War of 1812. It was his first voyage after he had been made midshipman and shortly after the United States had signed a treaty against slave trade. The President, who was a Virginian, still had some exaggerated feeling about putting an end to the horrible conditions of the slave trade. Once in a while something was done about it. Ingham's ship was for that reason in the South Atlantic. Ingham had thought that Nolan was a kind of layman acting as chaplain. At that time Ingham did not ask questions, because he would appear ignorant if he did. Everything aboard ship was strange to him and he thought that there was a man like Nolan on every ship. He was told not to say anything about home when Nolan dined in his mess once a week. It seemed to Ingham that it was only one more unreasonable request. He first came to understand Nolan when the ship captured a dirt schooner carrying slaves. The officer sent over to take charge of the slave ship asked that the captain send over someone who spoke Portuguese. Nolan said he understood Portuguese. He was sent over and Ingham went along with him.

Comment

Ingham attacks the failure of some presidents to work hard to put an end to the slave trade. He also describes his ignorance as a young midshipman and he gives his first impression of Nolan. Ingham expresses very strong feeling against slavery. President Abraham Lincoln freed the slaves by the Emancipation Proclamation of 1863 and slavery was one of the major causes of the Civil War that was being fought when Ingham wrote this story. Since 1808, by act of Congress, it was forbidden to import slaves, but illegal slave ships continued to violate this law. Both the United States and England agreed to put an end to this evil practice in 1814. Very soon the United States sent ships to the west coast of Africa to prevent further trade in slaves. Ingham feels that Presidents Jefferson, Madison, and Monroe did not work hard enough to stamp out the slave trade.

Ingham appears to have been very ignorant as a young man. He might, however, have been quite young. Admiral Farragut, for example, became a midshipman at the age of nine. Everything aboard ship is strange to Ingham and he does not understand why things are done. The presence of Nolan, therefore, does not seem unusual to him. Because Nolan wears a blue army coat without army buttons, Ingham imagines that he is a civilian who is substituting for the chaplain.

THE MAN WITHOUT A COUNTRY

TEXTUAL ANALYSIS

PART 5

TEXAS OUT OF THE MAP

Two officers from Texas, Waters and Williams, were at the table when Nolan asked about Texas. He had not heard anything about it for 20 years. He had heard about Honduras and Tamaulipas, and until recently about California where it seems his brother traveled and died. The two Texas men were embarrassed. So were two other officers. Nolan saw that something was wrong. Since Ingham was in command of the ship, he had to tell Nolan that Texas could not be discussed and he changed the subject.

Comment

Everyone is embarrassed by Nolan's question. That is why Waters and Williams look solemnly at one another and try not to laugh. That is why Edward Morris looks up at the third link in the chain on the chandelier. That is why Watrous begins to sneeze. None of them know what to do and no one can look at Nolan.

They know that Nolan will be embarrassed when he learns that he cannot talk about Texas. It means that there is another topic he cannot discuss. This topic he enjoyed discussing because it brought back happy memories of his brother and his own youth. Ingham says that Stephen Nolan died in California, but Danforth will write later that Stephen died in Texas.

Notes

Moses Austin (1761–1821) of Virginia got a grant of land from the Spanish government to settle 300 American families in Texas. His son, Stephen Fuller Austin (1793–1836), began settling thousands of American families in Texas in 1822. The Americans were dissatisfied with the Mexican administration of Texas and sent Austin to Mexico City of present their complaints. He was imprisoned there for a short time, but returned in 1835. When Texas became an independent republic in 1836, he was made Secretary of State.

Honduras is a Central American republic which won her independence from Spain in 1821.

Tamaulipas is a state in northeastern Mexico. It is just south of Texas. Nolan would not get news of this state when it was invaded by the United States in 1846.

California was a Spanish possession when Nolan was sentenced. He apparently knew that it was later part of Mexico when she became independent in 1821. American settlers set up an independent California republic in 1846 under the influence of the American General John C. Fremont. Mexico recognized the United States conquest of California by the Treaty of Guadalupe Hidalgo (1848), following the Mexican War. California became the 31st state in 1850. Nolan would not have gotten any news of California after Fremont's intervention there. He might not have gotten any news since 1841. In that year John Bidwell lead the first group of American settlers into California and Nolan would not be allowed to read about them.

Captain Back. Sir George Back (1796–1878) was an Englishman who explored northern Canada.

Sir Thomas Roe (1580–1644) was English ambassador to the Great Mogul of India from 1615 to 1619. Ingham begins talking about Back and Roe only to change the subject. Nolan's question about Texas had embarrassed everyone.

NOLAN GROWS OLD

Ingham never saw Nolan again. He wrote to him twice a year. They had become even more friendly and trusted one even more. Nolan aged very fast in the next 10 years, but he was always gentle. He never complained and he suffered his punishment in silence. He had brought it upon himself. He was somewhat less friendly with new men he did not know, but he was even more anxious to be a friend to the midshipmen and to help and teach them. Many seemed to worship him. Now he is dead and has found a home and country.

Comment

Earlier Nolan had shown physical courage in the frigate-duel. Now he shows a greater sort of courage in accepting without complaint his lifelong imprisonment. He serves his fellowmen and his country by instructing the young officer candidates.

Ingham suggests that Nolan has now found his home and country in heaven. He speaks of him with great affection. Ingham never saw Nolan again after the cruise on the George Washington. It appears that they met at least four times: (1) on the ship that caught the slave ship, about 1820–1822; (2) in 1830, but we are not told where; (3) about 1837 on the Intrepid, and (4) on the George Washington about 1841–6.

INGHAM RECEIVES LETTER FROM DANFORTH

After writing this sketch, Ingham wondered if he should print it. He thought it would be a warning to those who would betray their country as Nolan, Vallandigham, and Tattnall did. However, he decided to print the story when he got a letter from Danforth. Danforth gave an account of Nolan's last hours aboard the Levant.

Comment

Hale makes it clear that the moral of his patriotic tale is applied to events of his own time. Vallandigham and Tattnall were two men who, in Hale's opinion, betrayed their country. He finds them as guilty as Nolan was.

Notes

Clement Laird Vallandigham (1820–1871) was a United States Congressman from Ohio. He was a "Copperhead" or Democrat in the North who believed that the rights of the states were greater than those of the federal government. In 1863, when he was running for governor of Ohio, he gave a speech in which he expressed sympathy for the Confederate States. These states (Virginia, North Carolina,

South Carolina, Georgia, Tennessee, Alabama, Mississippi, Arkansas, Texas, Florida, and Louisiana) declared their independence from the United States in 1861 and the Civil War followed soon after. Because he gave this speech, Vallandigham was arrested and tried, just as Nolan was, by the United States Army. He was imprisoned in Fort Warren, tried by court-martial, and sentenced to be executed. President Lincoln changed the sentence to exile. He was conducted by troops to the border of the Confederate States. This incident gave Hale the main idea of his story. Both Nolan and Vallandigham were sent into exile because of treasonable statements. Vallandigham, however, was allowed to return to the United States in 1864 just as, much earlier, Aaron Burr was. Hale had hoped to have this story printed before the congressional election of 1863 so that it might help defeat Vallandigham. Through a series of accidents, the story did not appear until after the November elections, but Vallandigham was defeated anyhow.

Tatnall: This name should be spelled Tattnall. Josiah Tattnall (1795–1871) was a Commander in the United States Navy. When the Civil War broke out, however, he joined the Confederate Navy. His ship, the Merrimac (later called the Virginia) was a frigate that was covered with heavy sheets of iron. In March 9, 1862, his ship fought a Northern "iron-clad," the Monitor, at Hampton Roads, Virginia. This was a Northern victory and this conflict between two "iron-clad" ships changed the whole pattern of naval warfare. Hale obviously regards Tattnall as a traitor, because he took part in what Danforth later on calls "this infernal Rebellion."

NAVY PRETENDS THAT NOLAN DOES NOT EXIST

In order for those not in the Navy to understand the first part of Danforth's letter, it is necessary to understand that every officer who had charge of Nolan after 1817 was in a very awkward position. At that time the original order imprisoning Nolan was not renewed. A ship's captain in charge of Nolan, therefore, had no authority for keeping Nolan a prisoner. If Nolan had been freed, he might have sued that officer for kidnapping or false imprisonment. On the other hand, if the officer had let Nolan go free, the Navy might have tried him for violating the original order. When Ingham and others tried to get the Navy to do something about Nolan, they were told by Secretary of the Navy Southard that the officer in charge had to use his own judgment, that no new orders would be given. That meant that if an officer made the wrong decision, the Navy would not support him. The matter is closed, yet Ingham is afraid that he might be tried as a criminal for the evidence he gives in this story.

Comment

Ingham feels guilty because of his part in keeping Nolan a lifelong prisoner without specified orders. It is partly his fault, because he would not take a chance and release him. It is also the fault of the Navy Department, because the Secretary of the Navy refused to do anything and it was primarily his responsibility. Ingham also feels guilty, because he feels that Nolan had suffered too much and because Nolan was a friend of his.

Note

Samuel Lewis Southard (1787–1842) was Secretary of the Navy from 1823 to 1829, during the administrations of Presidents Monroe and John Quincy Adams. He should not be confused with W. Southard who is mentioned earlier.

NOLAN'S ROOM FILLED WITH REMINDERS OF AMERICA

Danforth writes to Ingham from the Levant. Nolan is now dead and Danforth understands why Ingham always spoke affectionately of him. His death came suddenly even though Danforth knew that Nolan was not well. The doctor told him that Nolan had not left his stateroom and that had never happened before. He even let the doctor into his stateroom for the first time. Danforth was asked to come to Nolan's room and he found him weak but happy. When Danforth and Ingham were young they used to make up stories about what secret things might be in Nolan's room. The American flag was hung from the wall, "triced up" about a picture of George Washington. Nolan had painted an American eagle on the wall. There was also a map of the United States, which he had drawn with odd old names on it. Texas was on the map and the American boundary went clear to the Pacific Ocean. He told Danforth that he was dying and that he was as loyal to the United States as any man. He knew that Burr's plot failed because there were 34 stars on the flag. He was sorry about his own desire for personal fame as a boy and said that states' rights ("separate sovereignty") was wrong. He asked Danforth to tell him everything about the United States before he died.

Comment

Until this moment no one knew anything about Nolan's stateroom. We now learn that they had for a long time filled his room with things that reminded him of his country. Because he is dying, he feels that he can ask Danforth to break the rules and tell him all the news from home. He has not heard anything for over 55 years. For the first time we are told that Nolan committed treason because he desired personal fame.

Notes

The Intrepid was an actual ship. Danforth and Ingham could not possibly have been on the original Intrepid, because it was sunk in 1804. Danforth must have been on the Intrepid when Ingham was the 2nd officer.

Majestic Eagle: This is the symbol of the United States. The lightning represents power and its foot clasping the whole globe represents American's strength throughout the world. Ingham wanted to see America expand to the Pacific Ocean. Nolan is delighted to learn that the nation has expanded that far.

Indiana Territory was organized in 1800. Indiana became the 19th state in 1816, nine years after Nolan's trial. This and other names are called "quaint, queer old names" because they are no longer used.

Mississippi Territory, when Nolan was sentenced, included both present-day Mississippi and Alabama. Mississippi became the 20th state in 1817 and Alabama the 22nd state in 1819.

Louisiana Territory was formed from the Louisiana Purchase in 1805. Five states had been carved out of this territory at the time of Nolan's death: Missouri (1821), 24th state; Arkansas (1836), 25th state; Iowa (1848), 29th state; Minnesota (1858), 32nd state; and Kansas (1861), 34th state.

Texas: Nolan realized that Texas has become either a state or a territory of the United States.

Pacific: The United States acquired title to present-day California, Arizona, Utah, Nevada, and parts of Colorado, Wyoming, and New Mexico as a result of the Mexican War. Title to present-day Washington, Oregon, Idaho was acquired by treaty with England in 1846.

DANFORTH TELLS NOLAN ABOUT WARS AND NEW STATES

Even though Danforth might have gotten into trouble for doing so, he promised to tell Nolan everything. He was sorry that he had not done so long before. Nolan asks about Captain Barron, David Porter, the Chesapeake, and the names of the new states. He knew about Ohio, Kentucky, and Tennessee, and had guessed that Michigan, Indiana, Mississippi, and Texas were also states. He was happy to hear about California. He tells Danforth that his brother died in Texas and he gave him a true account of the time he himself acted as gun captain aboard ship.

Comment

Danforth feels that Nolan has fully paid for ("expiated") his crime. He says that Nolan was a saint and, because he feels guilty for not having told him earlier about America, he tries very hard with great enthusiasm to tell him everything. Most of Danforth's letter is really a history of the United States from 1807 to 1863. Nolan, as a true patriot, is happy to learn about America's expansion.

Notes

A Tyrant is a cruel man who has absolute power as a ruler. Danforth is the captain of the Levant. The captain of the ship rules over everyone aboard. Danforth calls himself a tyrant, because he feels he has been cruel not to have told Nolan about America long before this.

Kentucky, the 15th state, was admitted to the Union in 1792. Nolan was born in Kentucky.

Tennessee, the 16th state, was admitted to the Union in 1796.

Ohio, the 17th state, was admitted to the Union in 1803.

Indiana, the 19th state, was admitted to the Union in 1816.

Mississippi, the 20th state, was admitted to the Union in 1817.

Michigan, the 26th state, was admitted to the Union in 1837.

California, the 31st state, admitted to the Union in 1850.

Oregon, the 33rd state, admitted to the Union in 1859.

Fort Adams. Nolan naturally recalls that Fort Adams is in Mississippi, because his trial was held there.

Texas, the 28th state, admitted to the Union in 1845.

Chesapeake: James Barron was commander of this ship when it was stopped at sea by the English ship Leopard in June, 1807. The English seized two English deserters and took two American citizens. At about the same time, Nolan was facing a court-martial, Barron was tried and dismissed from the Navy for failure to prepare his ship for combat. Nolan would not know the verdict.

David Porter and the Java. Nolan confirms the story Ingham told about the frigate-duel and he gives the name of the ship. He also asks about David Porter as he was confined to his ship, the Essex.

Other Fourteen: Nolan has counted 20 states, including Tennessee, and knows that there are 14 more. He is then told about Texas, California, and Oregon. The remaining eleven are: Louisiana (1812), 18th state; Illinois (1818), 21st state; Alabama (1819), 22nd state; Maine (1820), 23rd state; Missouri (1821), 24th state, Arkansas (1836), 25th state; Florida (1845), 27th state, Iowa (1846), 29th state; Wisconsin (1848), 30th state, Minnesota (1858), 32nd state; Kansas (1861), 34th state.

Text is a topic or subject. Nolan hopes that none of the older states were cut up. When Danforth says that "that is not a bad text," he means that he agrees with Nolan. Danforth does not know that Virginia was divided into two states. The western counties of Virginia refused to leave the Union when Virginia joined the Confederate States. These counties were admitted to the Union as the new state of West Virginia in June, 1863. It was the 35th state.

A Good Deal Besides Furs: In the early days, a great quantity or fur was exported from the Oregon Territory. Nolan means that the sailors came back from shore quite drunk.

NOLAN ASKS ABOUT THE "LEGION OF THE WEST"

Danforth regrets that he did not have more information, but he did the best he could. He told him about the War of 1812, Fulton's steamboat, General Scott, Andrew Jackson, Mississippi, New

Orleans, Texas, and Kentucky. Nolan asks who is in command of the "legion of the West" and Danforth tells him that Grant is.

Comment

Danforth tells Nolan everything he can think of about the United States since Nolan's imprisonment. However, when Nolan asks about the "legion of the West." He does not tell Nolan everything. It is true that Grant was at that time in Vicksburg as commander of the western Army. Danforth does not tell him that there is a Civil War and that Grant is invading the South.

Notes

English War is the War of 1812.

Robert Fulton (1765–1815) designed the first commercially successful steamboat, the Clermont. It was launched in 1807 and made a round trip between New York and Albany. After this, steamboats were built for travel on the great rivers of the United States.

General Winfield Scott (1786–1866) fought in the War of 1812 and Commander of the United States Army during the Mexican War.

General Andrew Jackson (1767–1845) fought in the War of 1812 and defeated the British army in the Battle of New Orleans. He was the 8th President of the United States (1829–1837).

General Ulysses S. Grant (1822–1885) was commander of the western division of the Army when Vicksburg was being attacked. He was later made Commander-in-Chief of the Army for the rest of the Civil War. After the war, he was elected President of the United States (1869–1877).

Vicksburg, Mississippi is located on the Mississippi River. It was settled in 1812 by Newitt Vick and named after him. Nolan remembers Vick's plantation. Grant seized Vicksburg on July 4, 1863, and cut the Confederate States in two.

Fort Adams was abandoned in 1819. It was located about 100 miles south of Vicksburg.

DANFORTH TELLS NOLAN ABOUT CHANGES IN THE UNITED STATES

Danforth does his best to tell Nolan about the movement of pioneers to the West, about steamboats, railroads, telegraphs, and other inventions. He tells him about books and literature and about the founding of West Point, Annapolis, and various colleges, and the Smithsonian Institution. He tells him about the statue, "Armed Liberty" that Crawford made, about Greenough's statue of Washington, and about the new Capitol Building. He tells him about the exploring expedition and his meeting with Harding, the Congressman from Oregon. He tells him nothing about the Civil War. Nolan is glad to hear that Lincoln does not come from an old and rich family and that he worked his now way up to the White House. Nolan asks many questions.

Comment

Danforth compares Nolan to a man who has been alone on a desert island for 56 years. Nolan knows about as much of what has taken place in the United States as such a man would. America grew very rapidly while Nolan was a prisoner aboard United States Navy ships. When he was sentenced, the population of the United States was about 7,000,000. At the time of his death it was about 23,000,000. In 1807, most Americans lived in the state bordering the Atlantic Ocean. In 1863, more than half of the population lived west of the Allegheny Mountains. There were also many inventions which changed America. For example, the railroad and the steamboat made it much easier to travel about the United States. The telegraph made it easy to send news about the country. Both Ingham and Nolan are opposed to the presidency being in the hands of certain old and rich families. That is why Nolan is so happy to hear that Abraham Lincoln is President even though he never heard of him before.

Notes

Emigration means the movement of settlers from the East to the West and the Far-West. They usually traveled by covered wagon, also called Conestoga wagon after the town in Pennsylvania where they were manufactured.

Steamboats: Danforth already told him about the Clermont. He would then have to tell him that steamboats were used for transporting passengers and freight on most large rivers.

Railroads: The first steam-driven locomotive to pull a load of passengers appeared in the United States in 1830. Railroads grew rapidly and six years after Nolan died they stretched from coast to coast.

Telegraph: Samuel Finley Breese Morse (1791–1872) invented the telegraph in 1832 and the first commercial telegraph line was opened in 1844. By the time of the Civil War, the telegraph was widely used throughout the country.

Inventions: Some of the inventions of this period were the reaper, sewing machine, submarine, and Bessemer steel process.

Books And Literature: While Nolan was a prisoner, a large number of great writers appeared in America. Of the 13 great writers of this period, Nolan could have heard of only one. That was Washington Irving (1783–1863). He wrote a few minor things before Nolan was sentenced, but Nolan could not have read his "Rip Van Winkle" or "The Legend of Sleepy Hollow." The other great writers of this period are: William Cullen Bryant (1794–1878), James Fenimore Cooper (1789–1851), Ralph Waldo Emerson (1803–1882), Nathaniel Hawthorne (1804–1864), Oliver Wendell Holmes (1809–1894), James Russell Lowell (1819–1891), Henry Wadsworth Longfellow (1807–1882), Herman Melville (1819–1891), Edgar Allan Poe (1809–1849), Henry David Thoreau (1817–1862), Walt Whitman (1819–1892), and John Greenleaf Whittier (1807–1892).

West Point: The United States Military Academy at West Point, a training school for Army officers, was established in 1802. Nolan would have heard about this before he was made a prisoner.

Navy School: The United States Naval Academy at Annapolis, Maryland was established in 1845. It was first called the United States Naval School.

Colleges: A large number of colleges and universities were established in the country during Nolan's period of imprisonment.

For example, New York University was established in 1831, the University of Virginia in 1819, Haverford and Oberlin in 1833, the University of Wisconsin in 1848, and Vassar in 1861.

Robinson Crusoe is a novel by Daniel Defoe (1660–1731). The hero of this novel was shipwrecked on a desert island for over 28 years.

Old Abe is a nickname for Abraham Lincoln (1809–1865), the 16th President of the United States (1860–1865). He was born in Kentucky just as Nolan was. He grew up in Indiana and later he moved to Illinois. His family were poor frontier people and he was largely self-educated. He worked at many jobs, studied law, became a lawyer, was elected to Congress, and in 1860 he became President.

General Benjamin Lincoln (1733–1810) fought in the Revolutionary War and was later Secretary of War (1781–1783). Nolan says that he once met General Lincoln and admired him, but he is glad to learn that "Old Abe" is not his son.

Oregon Congressman Harding: Benjamin Franklin Harding (1823–1899) was United States Senator from Oregon from September 1862 to March 1865.

Smithsonian: The Smithsonian Institution was established in Washington, D.C. by an act of Congress. It was made possible by a grant of more than 100,000 English pounds to the United States Government by James Smithson (1765–1829), an Englishman who had never visited the United States. It is principally a museum of zoology and ethnology. It also has a great astrophysical observatory.

Exploring Expedition: The most famous exploring expedition of this period is that of Lewis and Clark (1803-1806). The Zebulon Pike Expedition (1806-1807) was also well known. John C. Fremont lead an exploring expedition to California and other western areas in 1843 and in 1845.

Crawford's Liberty. Thomas Crawford (1813-1857), an American sculpture, designed the "Armed Liberty" which stands on the dome of the Capitol in Washington. It is also called "Armed Freedom."

Greenough's Washington. Horatio Greenough (1805-1852) designed a huge statue of George Washington for the Capitol Building. It was too heavy, however, and now rests in the Smithsonian Institution. Greenough made Washington look like an Olympian god.

Infernal Rebellion. The Civil War.

NOLAN'S LAST PRAYERS AND HIS LAST REQUEST

Nolan listens carefully and with pleasure to all that Danforth tells him. He becomes quiet and then asks for a glass of water. He has Danforth read him two prayers from the Book of Public Prayer. One prayer is for the United States, the President, and all who have authority. The other is a prayer of thanks. He tells Danforth that he has said those two prayers every morning and evening for 55 years. He pulls Danforth towards him and gives him a fatherly kiss. He asks Danforth to look in his Bible after he is dead. Danforth then leaves Nolan's stateroom. Nolan appeared happy and Danforth thought that he wanted to rest. In less than an hour, the doctor finds that Nolan is dead. Resting on his lips is his father's badge of the Order of Cincinnati. Danforth opens Nolan's

Bible to a place which Nolan had indicated with a piece of paper. Nolan had placed a mark next to one verse. The verse reads: "They desire a country, even a heavenly [country]: wherefore God is not ashamed to be called their God: for he hath prepared for them a city." On the piece of paper Nolan wrote that he wanted a stone in his memory set up either in New Orleans or at Fort Adams. The inscription is to read: "In memory of Philip Nolan, Lieutenant in the Army of the United States. He loved his country as no other man has loved her. But no man deserved less at her hands."

Comment

Philip Nolan seemed to have had a sad life. He died happy, however. He was happy because he learned that the United States had expanded and become prosperous. He was happy because no one had succeeded in dividing the United States. He was happy because, after he had admitted to himself that it was wrong to have betrayed his country, he spent the rest of his life praying for her and serving her as best he could. His request that he be buried at sea like a sailor indicates that he had long ago come to accept his life at sea. He did not feel that he was a prisoner any longer. He is also happy because, through the promise of his religion, he expects to find his true "country" in heaven. Nolan has actually found that he has a country and that is why he wants the monument set up in New Orleans or at Fort Adams. He is not really, now, a man without a country.

Notes

The Book Of Public Prayer that Danforth is referring to is the Directory of Public Worship used in Presbyterian services at this time.

Episcopal Collect. A collect is a short, formal prayer used in public worship. There are a number of such prayers in The Book of Common Prayer used by the Protestant Episcopal Church of the United States. Danforth, who seems to be an Episcopalian, notices that the collect that Nolan has him read from the Directory of Public Worship is very much like one in *The Book of Common Prayer.*

Order Of Cincinnati. This patriotic organization of officers who had fought in the Revolutionary War was founded in 1783. It is correctly called the Society of the Cincinnati. Today its members are the descendants of the original founders of the society.

Biblical Text. These lines from the Bible are taken from St. Paul's Epistle to the Hebrews, chapter 11, verse 16.

THE MAN WITHOUT A COUNTRY

ANALYSES OF CHARACTERS

Philip Nolan

Philip Nolan was a proud, undisciplined, quick-tempered young man who was eager to earn fame. His father fought in the Revolutionary War. Philip was born in Kentucky and raised on a plantation. He met few educated Americans, but he met a number of French merchants and Spanish officers. Even when his father once hired a tutor for him, the tutor was an Englishman. Philip learned very little about his own country. He frequently hunted wild horses with his brother in Texas. He enlisted in the Army, but found Army life dull. He readily joined Burr's plot, because he wanted to earn fame. He lost his temper when he was being tried for treason. He was too proud and self-confident to treat the sentence of the court seriously. He suffers then a series of embarrassments which prove that he is truly in prison.

Nolan changes his character shortly after he realizes that he will be a prisoner for the rest of his life. He no longer acts in a proud fashion and he becomes shy. He learns to love his country, he becomes religious and kind, and he learns to accept his hard life. He had sought fame and later when he learns that people do not even know his name, he does not complain. He proves his bravery and devotion to his country in a frigate-duel. On his death bed he says that he has prayed most of his life for his country. He has sympathy for Negroes and others who suffer. He takes a fatherly interest in the young midshipmen aboard his ship. He had been bored with the dull life in an Army camp. On board ship, where there is even less freedom and fewer things to do, he organizes a life-long program of reading and study and he leads a contented life.

Frederic Ingham

Called "Fred" or "Ingham" in this story, but in other stories his full name is given as Frederic Ingham. He appears first as an ignorant young midshipman, but he is very much impressed with Nolan and, because Nolan is kind to him, he becomes a devoted friend to him. He works hard to get Nolan released. At the time of Nolan's death, he is a retired Navy officer, probably around 60 years old. He prides himself on his memory, but he often forgets. He is very honest and tries to tell the truth about Nolan. He feels guilty for his part in Nolan's imprisonment.

Danforth

The captain of the Levant at the time of Nolan's death. He has known Nolan for many years and has a strong affection for him. He feels guilty for his part in withholding news of the United States from Nolan. He is a close friend of Nolan. Both served aboard the Intrepid when Nolan was on that ship.

Aaron Burr

An historical person, but he is very important in this work of fiction. As depicted by Ingham, Burr is a dishonest, light-hearted, and ruthless man. He is responsible for Nolan's treason and imprisonment. His brilliance attracts Nolan, but he only contacts Nolan when he feels he can use him. Burr does not feel guilty because of his treason. On his death bed, Nolan is able to say that he forgives Burr.

IDENTIFICATION OF MINOR CHARACTERS

William Bainbridge

He is simply called the "Commodore" in the incident of the frigate-duel. He was captain of the Constitution. He thanked Nolan for his part in the fight and gave Nolan his own dress sword and reported Nolan's bravery to the Secretary of the Navy.

Harry Cole

A Navy officer who thinks Texas should be cut out of Nolan's maps.

Dick

Leader of the Negro band aboard the Warren.

Mrs. Graff

Miss Rutledge before she married. She dances with Nolan aboard the Warren. She knows his sentence and will not speak to him about home.

Lieutenant Mitchell

The officer, probably a Navy officer, in New Orleans to whom Nolan is turned over by the Army.

Colonel Morgan

An old man and a Revolutionary War veteran. He is chief judge at court-martial of Nolan. His patriotism is shocked when Nolan curses the United States.

Edward Morris

He aboard the George Washington when Nolan asks about Texas. He looks at chandelier because he is embarrassed.

Stephen Nolan

The older brother of Philip. He used to hunt wild horses with Philip in Texas. He died in Texas before 1807.

Phillips

He borrowed *The Lay of the Last Minstrel* from an English surgeon. He told Ingham how Nolan lost his temper and threw this book into the ocean.

George Pons

He knew little about history, thought Nolan was "Junius."

Davis Porter

An historical person. Nolan was with him aboard the Essex when he seized the Nuku-Hiva Islands. He asked about him on his death bed.

Captain Shaw

Commander of the Nautilus. Ingham is not quite sure of this, however. He tore *The Tempest* from Nolan's copy of the works of Shakespeare.

Shubrick

He was guarding Nolan when he slipped away and danced with Mrs. Graff.

W. Southard

He signed the original letter of instructions regarding Nolan on behalf of the Secretary of the Navy.

Tingey

At first Ingham is not sure whether Tingey or Shaw was commander of the Nautilus. He later decides it was Shaw.

Lieutenant Truxton

He told Ingham about the officers who discussed whether or not to cut Texas out of Nolan's maps.

Tucker

Ingham thinks that either Tucker or Watson had charge of Nolan at the end of the War of 1812.

Vaughan

He is the officer who was put in charge of a captured slave ship. He has Nolan act as his translator. He is a sympathetic and emotional man.

Waters and Williams

They are Navy officers from Texas. Nolan's question about Texas embarrasses them.

Watrous

He sneezes to hide his embarrassment when Nolan asks about Texas.

Watson

Ingham thinks that either Watson or Tucker had charge of Nolan at the end of the War of 1812.

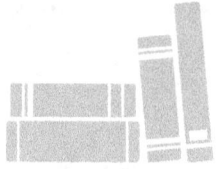

THE MAN WITHOUT A COUNTRY

CRITICAL REVIEW

CONSIDERED A CLASSIC

Edward Everett Hale's patriotic short story is considered to be an American classic. It has faults in structure and its basic situation is almost unbelievable. Nevertheless, Hale has Ingham relate the tale in such a realistic fashion that it appears to be simple historical truth.

PATRIOTISM

Hale wrote his story in the first place out of love of country. In 1863, Clement L. Vallandigham of Ohio said that he would rather not live in a country that was being governed by Abraham Lincoln. This shocked Hale so much that he wrote this story to help defeat Vallandigham in the fall election of that year. Hale, like Colonel Morgan who sentenced Nolan, believed that love of country is a natural and sacred duty. He wrote his novel while the United States was engaged in the Civil War. He wished to protect the American Union and throughout the story he attacks

Burr, Tattnall, and other traitors to the United States. *The Man Without a Country*, tells the story of a young man who betrays his country. However, when he is kept away from his country, he comes to learn that love of country is more important than any personal interest.

The story has many "sermons" or "lessons" on patriotism. For example, Nolan gives Ingham what is in effect a sermon on patriotism after they leave the slave ship. These sermons slow down the story and are not so very convincing. The reader is convinced by the story and the character of Philip Nolan. He becomes a lonely, pitiful, and strange man, because he lacked patriotism; He cuts himself off from his country, his family, and his home. He lacks the very things that most men take for granted. His situation is very unusual. It is doubtful if any man ever received such a sentence. What he experiences, however, are emotions that all men experience, no matter their race, language, or country. Most men know what it is to be homesick. Nolan is homesick all his life, it seems. For that reason he fills his stateroom with reminders of home. It is natural for men who are away from home to talk about it. Nolan arouses our pity because he is not even permitted to do this. Men do not feel at ease with him, because they are then forbidden to talk about the things that interest most men: home, family, and country. This makes Nolan appear even more lonely and strange. Hale's patriotic subject is successful because it is, for the most part, presented in the concrete figure of Philip Nolan. His story teaches the value of patriotism, because we see how empty and lonely life is for men who lack this value. Clifton Fadiman says that "no story better expresses the spirit of American nationalism." The patriotism or nationalism that Hale presents was not always a part of American life. Before the American Revolution men gave their loyalty to England and the English king. Americans were bitterly divided during the American Revolution on the question of patriotism. The loyalists believed that patriotic feelings should be given to England. The revolutionaries believed that patriotic feelings should be given to the land in which men lived. The War of 1812 increased American patriotism and the issue of national patriotism was finally decided during the Civil War.

STRUCTURE

In a short story there are not usually many characters or events (episodes) and the story is usually a simple one. This is not true of *The Man Without a Country*. Hale has Ingham (with Danforth's help) tell all the important **episodes** in the life of Philip Nolan. He tells them in a very complicated fashion. For example, Ingham at one point relates what some officers told him when he was in Egypt around 1820 or 1822. Then he goes back to the years between 1807 and 1810 to tell about Nolan's reading *The Lay of the Last Minstrel*. Ingham does not tell his story in chronological order. There are many episodes. For example, the meeting with Mrs. Graff, the capture of the slave ship, Nolan's heroism aboard the Constitution, and the conversation about Texas when Ingham was captain of the ship to which Nolan was attached. A complicated plot of many episodes, with movements back and forth in time, is more appropriate to a novel than to a short story.

A story usually has a **climax** or a single point of high interest. Often the problem presented in the story may be explained or solved after the **climax**. There is no single high point in *The Man Without a Country*. There are at least three high points after the trial of Philip Nolan. They are the meeting with Mrs. Graff, the capture of the slave ship, and the gift of the sword to Nolan by Captain William Bainbridge. The meeting with Mrs. Graff finally breaks Nolan's pride and convinces him that he is truly in "prison." The capture of the slave ship shows that Nolan is terribly homesick and, indeed, loves his country. The gift of the sword gives momentary hope than Nolan may be set free. There is not much suspense, however. We know from the beginning, that Nolan died in "prison." These three **episodes** do not build up to a single high point or **climax**. Danforth's letter to Ingham clears up a small mystery and gives some surprise at the end. Short story writers like the French Guy de Maupassant and the American O. Henry give an unexpected or ironic ending to their stories. There is nothing ironic in Hale's ending, however, Nolan's stateroom was mysterious, because no one was ever allowed to enter it. Both Ingham and Danforth had been curious about it when young. Danforth clears up this minor mystery when he describes the stateroom to Ingham in his letter. Early in the story, the reader learns that Nolan regretted his treason, loved his country, and became adjusted to his imprisonment. He appeared always sad and lonely. Danforth surprises the reader to a certain extent when he tells Ingham that Nolan was finally happy aboard ship.

All these scattered **episodes** are united around the figure of Nolan and made subordinate to the one situation. The one situation is Nolan's life-long exile at sea for treason and the forbidding of any mention of the United States to him.

REALISM

"**Realism**" as used here has nothing to do with a literary movement of the same name. Here "**realism**" means an attempt by the writer to describe things just as they are. Edward Everett Hale, Jr. said that the plot of his father's story is "grotesque." That is, the plot is not like anything we would expect in real life. Hale, however, makes the story "realistic" or believable by his careful attention to detail. For example, Ingham tells the reader exactly where he was when he read about Nolan's death. He quotes the announcement, gives the name of the newspaper, and the date. When he tells about a trip from Alexandria to Cairo, he says that he traveled by donkey, but that today camels are used for the same trip. Even the mistakes that Ingham makes are part of this "realism." He is an old, retired, Navy captain and has trouble remembering all the names and the order of events. Carl van Doren says, "he writes for the most part like a sailor, plainly with the desire to get to the truth and tell nothing else." Hale's use of historical persons and events also contribute to his **realism**. For example, Aaron Burr, Jefferson, and Austin are real people. The War of 1812 and the Civil War are historical events.

It has already been pointed out that Hale gave a number of hints to his readers that his story is not true. For example, he has Ingham write that Nolan died on the Levant in 1863. That very ship was lost at sea somewhere in the Pacific Ocean in 1861 and its disappearance was reported in the American newspapers. In spite of such hints, Hale's readers were often convinced that Philip Nolan was a real person. Many people, for example, reported to Hale that they had met his Philip Nolan.

Hale made two attempts to convince the public that his Philip Nolan was a fictional character. He discovered that there was a real Philip Nolan. He was a friend of General James Wilkinson. Wilkinson was an associate of Aaron Burr, but he testified against him. The real Philip Nolan was killed by the Spaniards near Waco, Texas in 1801. In *The Man Without a Country*, Philip Nolan has a brother Stephen who died in Texas. In 1876, Hale published a novel called Philip Nolan's Friends. It was based on the life of the real Philip Nolan. In 1901, Hale published an article called "The Real Philip Nolan" in a scholarly journal. Both have been neglected. It is Hale's fictional Philip Nolan which still survives. This is because he made him believable. Hale wrote this story to influence an election campaign in 1863 and to rally support for the Union during the Civil War. His story became immediately popular and made him famous. Van Wyck Brooks says that *The Man Without a Country* "has been accepted generally as an American classic."

VOCABULARY OF NAVAL AND MILITARY TERMS

Ark: Large, flat-bottom boats used on the Mississippi River.

Artillery: Army unit which uses large guns or cannons.

Berth: Bunk or bed aboard ship.

Captain: In the Navy this rank is just below commodore and above commander. It is also the title of any officer who is in command of a ship. In the Army this rank is just below major and above lieutenant.

Captain of a gun: One in charge of a cannon or large gun.

Cockpit: Space or room just below the waterline of a ship. It is used for the wounded during battle. At other times it is used for junior officers.

Colonel: Army rank just below brigadier or brigadier general and above lieutenant colonel.

Commodore: Navy rank just below rear admiral and above captain.

Corvette: Warship which used to carry one row of guns, 20 or less, on its main deck. It was smaller than a frigate.

Court-martial: Army or Navy court which tries service men according to military law.

Cruise: Sea voyage. In Nolan's time, a cruise usually lasted three years.

Flatboat: Large river boat with flat bottom.

Frigate: Ordinary warship which carried between 30 and 40 cannons. Cannons fired from both the main deck and ports beneath main deck.

Lieutenant: In the Navy this rank is just below lieutenant commander and above lieutenant (junior grade). In the Army first lieutenant is the rank just below captain and above second lieutenant.

Man-of-war: Warship or armed vessel.

Marshal: Military officer in charge of prisoners.

Mess: Place where meals are served. Men who dine together. The meal served to a group of men.

Midshipman: Boy or young man who worked aboard ship to train to become an officer. Today a midshipman takes his training at the United States Naval Academy at Annapolis, Maryland.

Outward bound: Traveling away from the home port.

Packet: Ship which carried passengers and mail. They were usually small and had three masts.

Port: Porthole or small opening in side of ship for admitting air and light or for shooting a weapon through. Also the left side of a ship as one faces the bow or front of the ship.

Quarters: Place where service men live.

Quarter-deck: Back or rear part of the upper deck. It is reserved for officers.

Rammer: Rod or ramrod used to drive home charge for muzzle-loading gun.

Rations: Food for one person for one day.

Ravelins: V-shaped fortification or defensive dike.

Raw hands: Sailors lacking experience either in battle or on the sea.

Round shot: A single shot.

Salt-junk: Salt meat used aboard ship.

Schooner: A ship with two or more masts. It has fore - and aft-rigged sails. That is, sails appear to be flat when seen from side.

Skiff: Light open boat, usually rowed, but sometimes sails used.

Smoking deck: Because Navy ships carry explosives, smoking is permitted only at specified places.

Stateroom: Private room with bed or bunk aboard ship.

Stockade: Protective enclosure made of upright poles or stakes.

Traps: Personal possessions or luggage.

Watch: In the Navy, officers and men are divided into groups or watches. Also period of time assigned each division or watch to guard and man ship. A watch usually lasts four hours.

Watering place: Any place where sailors may obtain fresh water.

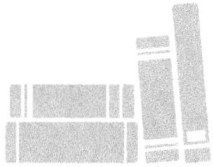

THE MAN WITHOUT A COUNTRY

ESSAY QUESTIONS AND ANSWERS

Question: What is the "Legion of the West"?

Answer: It has two meanings in Hale's story. First of all, it means the western division of the army around the year 1807. The Army governed the as yet unorganized territories of the Louisiana Purchase. It also guarded the border facing Spanishheld West Florida and Texas. Nolan was a lieutenant in this "Legion" when he was arrested and tried for his part in the Aaron Burr Plot. Secondly, it means the western division of the Army under the command of General Ulysses S. Grant. At the time of his death, Nolan asks who is in command of this division. Danforth tells him that Grant is. He does not tell him however, that Grant had just seized Vicksburg and that there is a war between the North and South.

Question: What is Middle Passage?

Answer: Middle Passage is the slave-trade traffic from western Africa to the West Indies. In 1808 the United State forbade any further importation of slaves. This law was frequently violated, however. The United States and England, in the Treaty of Ghent of 1814, agreed to do all in their power to put an end to this trade. Philip Nolan was aboard a ship of the United States Navy assigned to the west coast of Africa to prevent this trade. Ingham, who was aboard the same ship, describes the filth and misery and human suffering connected with slave ships. He blames presidents who were born in Virginia for not doing enough to put an end to the slave trade. Nolan acts as translator to let the slaves know that they are free.

Question: What is "separate sovereignty"?

Answer: This is the doctrine that holds that each state has the same separate power of a free nation. When 11 Southern states claimed that they had this right and left the Union, the Civil War followed because the rest of the country denied that they had this right. The Civil War lasted from 1861 to 1865. Both Nolan and Ingham disagree with this doctrine. Vallandigham, an Ohio politician, is called a traitor for supporting this doctrine. Aaron Burr did not proclaim this doctrine, but he did plan to remove some western territories from United Stated control. Hale holds that no state or territory has the right to leave the United States.

Question: What excuse can you make for Nolan's treason?

Answer: Nolan knew very little about the United States that he was serving. He was brought up in the area around Kentucky and Louisiana. Louisiana at that time was a Spanish possession but most of the people there were French. The guests at his father's home were French or Spanish. There is no evidence that he visited other parts of the country as a boy. He did take hunting trips to Texas, which was a Spanish territory, as a young man. He had only one teacher and he was foreigner, an Englishman. He acquired more learning when he made a trip on business to Vera

Cruz, Mexico. Nolan was also bored with the dull life in the army post to which he was attached and Burr offered him excitement.

Question: Why was Nolan's sentence of lifelong imprisonment never remitted?

Answer: It was never withdrawn because of the red tape in the Navy Department in Washington. The original instructions governing Nolan were set up in 1807 and every officer in charge of Nolan kept these instructions and followed them. Nolan's file in Washington was supposedly lost when the English set fire to that city. No one in any of the offices of the Navy wanted to "stick his neck out" and make a decision about Nolan. It was the responsibility of the Secretary of the Navy to do this. But he told Ingham and others that he would not issue orders and that they would have to use their own judgment in handling Nolan. At other times the Navy Department would simply say that they knew nothing about Nolan. If a captain of a ship to which Nolan was attached let him go free, he might be found guilty of disobeying orders. If Nolan ever got free, he might sue those captains for kidnapping him or for false imprisonment. No one did anything, because they were afraid of getting into trouble. Nolan was a victim of government red tape.

Question: How did Danforth violate his orders?

Answer: Danforth was the captain of the Levant at the time of Nolan's death. He had aboard the ship the original instructions governing Nolan. They had been approved by President Jefferson. He was forbidden to let Nolan hear of the United States. Yet he told Nolan all that he could think of about the United States and all that had happened since 1807. He even drew in the rest of the states of the Union on his maps.

Question: What did Nolan have in common with Linnaeus?

Answer: Both were interested in "natural science" and both liked to classify according to scientific principles. Linnaeus established the classification for plants. Nolan devotes scrapbooks to plants and animals. He classifies them by their scientific names.

Question: Was Nolan an educated man?

Answer: Nolan did not have much education when he was in the Army. He had only one teacher and that for a period of less than a year. It is likely, however, that he knew both French and Spanish at this time. During his period of imprisonment, he read and studied for a set period each day. For example, he read the plays of Shakespeare, the Bible, and Flechier's sermons. He took notes on his reading and kept several scrapbooks. He would also have learned a great deal when officers took turns reading aloud to one another. He knew a great deal about ships for he taught midshipmen about them. He knew mathematics and taught this subject to Ingham. He had learned a great deal about guns while in the Army. If Ingham is correct in saying that Nolan knew Portuguese, he must have learned that language while aboard ship.

Question: Why does Danforth not tell Nolan that the Civil War is in progress?

Answer: Because he wants Nolan to die happy. Nolan himself had been corrupted by Aaron Burr who tried to tear parts of the United States away and establish an empire for himself. In his imprisonment, Nolan learned that he was wrong to have helped Burr. Nolan was happy to learn that man states had been added to the Union and that America stretched from the Atlantic to the

Pacific. It would make Nolan very unhappy then to learn that 11 states had broken away from the Union and that a great war was being fought between two sections of the country.

Question: How many examples of Nolan's quick-temper do we find in this book?

Answer: We know of three times that Nolan becomes angry for he is quick-tempered by nature. At his trial for treason he loses his temper and curses the United States. He says he would like never to hear of it again. He loses his temper a second time because he is embarrassed. While reading aloud from *The Lay of the Last Minstrel* he finds that the passage he is reading speaks with pity of a man without a country. Nolan is such a man. He throws the book into the sea. He becomes angry on his death bed. When Burr's name is mentioned, Nolan grinds his teeth together in anger because he remembers his own treason and what Burr did to him. However, he quickly recovers and says that he has forgiven Burr. Danforth says that he had never seen Nolan angry before. This indicates that Nolan had learned to control his temper.

Question: How would Nolan know the number of states in the Union?

Answer: He would know by looking at the flag of the United States which flies aboard every ship of the Navy. There were 17 stars on the flag and 17 states when Nolan was sentenced in 1807. At the time of his death there were 34 stars on the flag flying from the Levant. Actually there were 35 states in the Union at that time, but news had not yet reached the ship. West Virginia was the 35th state.

Question: Why is *The Man Without a Country* called a **didactic** story?

Answer: A **didactic** story teaches a lesson or a moral. Hale teaches in this story the importance of patriotism or the love for country. A didactic story, like a good sermon, gives an example of the lesson it teaches. That example is Philip Nolan. He learned that it is natural for a man to love and serve his country and that a man cannot be happy without a country that he loves.

Question: Which presidents does Ingham criticize?

Answer: Ingham criticizes the Presidents from Virginia. He had three reasons for criticizing them. (1) He felt that they did not do enough to put an end to the slave trade. (2) He did not think it right that all the presidents should come from the same state and from rich, well-established families. Nolan agrees with him when he says that he is happy that Abraham Lincoln came from a poor family and that he worked his own way up to the presidency. (3) Ingham wanted to see the United States expand. For example, he wanted the United States to obtain a watering place in the Pacific. At that time the United States did not own any islands in the Pacific. Porter temporarily held Nuku-Hiva for the United States and even renames the main island after President Madison. The Presidents who were from Virginia did not show any interest in expansion into the Pacific. The United States did not hold on to Nuku-Hiva and it later became a possession of France. Hawaii did not become an American possession until 1898.

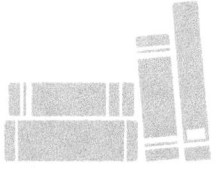

BIBLIOGRAPHY

WORKS BY EDWARD EVERETT HALE

The Man Without a Country. Boston: J. Stilman Smith & Co., Publishers, 1891. Introduction by Hale.

The Man Without a Country. New York: Heritage Press, 1936. Introduction by Carl Van Doren.

"Philip Nolan and the Levant," *National Geographic*, XVI (March, 1905), 114–6.

"The Real Philip Nolan," *Mississippi Historical Society Publications*, IV (1901), 281–329.

The Life and Letters of Edward Everett Hale. ed. Edward E. Hale, Jr. 2 Vols. Boston: Little Brown and Company, 1917.

Memories of a Hundred Years. New York: Macmillan Company, 1902.

WORKS ABOUT EDWARD EVERETT HALE

Brooks, Van Wyck. *New England: Indian Summer 1865–1915*. New York: E. P. Dutton and Co., Inc., 1940.

Frothington, Paul Revere. "Memoir of Edward Everett Hale," *Proceedings of the Massachusetts Historical Society*, LV (1923), 307–318.

Higginson, T. W. "Edward Everett Hale." *Outlaw*, LXXXXII (1906), 403–6.

Holloway, Jean. *Edward Everett Hale: A Biography*. Austin: University of Texas Press, 1956. This is the best work on Hale.

Pattee, Fred L. "The Short Story" in *Cambridge History of American Literature*. Ed. W. P. Trent et al. New York: The Macmillan Company, 1918.

Quinn, Arthur Hobson. *The Literature of the American People: An Historical and Critical Survey*. New York: Appleton-Century-Crofts, Inc., 1951.

www.ingramcontent.com/pod-product-compliance
Lightning Source LLC
LaVergne TN
LVHW011722060526
838200LV00051B/2992